The Time Retriever

What Will You Do With The Extra Hours In Your Day?

BY PETER JOHNSON

I dedicate this book to my wife Suzanne for all of her loving support over the years, and to my sons Nathan, Andrew and Karl.

A special thank you to Cydney O'Sullivan and Carrie Myton and the team at Motivational Speakers International for all of the publishing work.

Kylie Short at Tilda Virtual and Barb Scott at Admin Angels for their proofreading, editing and book development.

WriteItClearly.com for editing and proof reading.

"Successful People Don't Have Time and Then Plan, They Have Time Because They Plan"

ABOUT

This book is about helping business owners and managers to get control of their day-to-day working life. However, it can also be used by anyone looking to create more success in their life.

I have written it so that you can work through each step of the planning process, one at a time, using the templates provided at the back of the book. You can then use the second part of the book to help eliminate Procrastination, Interruptions and Distractions in your day.

It was written as a result of coaching business owners for nearly 9 years and over 30 years of business management and people management experience.

It is meant to be a resource that can be reviewed over and over again, because getting control of your time will not happen overnight (there is no magic that makes this happen immediately). You will need to develop and grow your skills constantly.

My recommendation is that you find someone who has the skills to help you develop your time management knowledge and skills, and more importantly, keep you accountable for doing what you plan to do.

I hope you enjoy using this resource and gain a lot of success from using it.

Remember, this material can only increase your knowledge; you actually have to action what you learn to make it work.

Peter Johnson

CONTENTS

4 INESCAPABLE COMPONENTS OF TIME MANAGEMENT

1. PLANNING
2. TIME MANAGEMENT
3. SELF-DISCIPLINE
4. PEOPLE MANAGEMENT SKILLS

Without knowledge and skills in each of these four components, you will always struggle to manage your time and achieve the goals you have set for your business and your life.

1. PLANNING

Time management is impossible if you don't have a plan. The plan determines what activities are important to you and therefore have to be done first to achieve your goals in business and life. With a plan, you know where to best use your time.

Steps to building your plan

a. **Why** – The planning process is about understanding why you do what you do. Understanding the why is very important to help you do and achieve what is really important to you and to keep you focused during the tough times.

b. **Vision** – The vision is the picture that you have in your head of what you want to achieve. Get it out on paper – it helps to clarify and solidify what you want to achieve.

c. **Goals/Targets** – Your main goals come from your vision; they are the targets you are looking for to achieve your vision. You can set your goals over 1, 3, 5, 10, or 20 year time frames. However, if that seems unrealistic to you, just set yourself some goals for the next 12 months and focus on building a plan to achieve them.

d. **Quarterly Action Plan** – This is the point where planning starts to cross into time management. In a quarterly action plan, you create a plan for the next 3 months. In this plan you set your goals for the quarter and each month of the quarter. You then set the activities that you will action in each week of the month to achieve those goals.

2. TIME MANAGEMENT

Time management is about setting your plans on a weekly and daily basis, determining on which day and time activities will be carried out.

a. **Weekly Planning** – Using your quarterly action plan and diary system, you planwhich day activities from the action plan are to be completed. You also plan in your appointments, family, social and any other activities you intend to carry out in that week.

b. **Daily Planning** – This is about scheduling in your activities for the day, creating a To Do List that you prioritise, and then following those priorities no matter what. How you set your prioritisation of this list is very important; the way most courses teach you to prioritise is wrong and results in only today-focused tasks to be completed and goals not achieved. Our method of prioritising tasks each day results in our clients getting more of the important activities actually completed on time.

3. SELF-DISCIPLINE

Without self-discipline, creating new and better time management skills simply will not happen. The process has to start from within you.

a. **Avoiding Procrastination** – There are many excuses for why we put off doing things, but the simple fact is that each time we avoid doing something that is important we are destroying our success. We need to learn how to control the way we think about various activities and complete them in their sequence of importance.

b. **Distractions** – An inability to stay focused on an important activity for a pre-set amount of time prevents us from achieving the success we want. Allowing ourselves to be constantly distracted by an array of things such as emails, phone calls, SMS, new apps, new technology, social media, new shiny bright things, etc., etc. means it just takes longer and longer to do things.

Each time you are distracted from doing something important, it takes 10 to 20 minutes to get back to the presence you had before you were distracted. You need to create a methodology for how you let yourself be distracted for short periods of time in between the important activities.

4. PEOPLE MANAGEMENT SKILLS

One of the biggest road blocks to achieving good time management skills and habits is interruptions from other people: team members, customers, suppliers, family, etc. It's important that you identify what interrupts you during your day, and create an action plan to eliminate those interruptions.

There is a lot to learn about managing people; however, from a time management perspective, there are some key things you need to learn that will help you get back hours in your day.

a.   Learn to teach your employees how to solve their own problems and make the decisions you pay them to make, instead of coming to you all the time. If you are someone that requires employees to come to you for decisions and not make them themselves, you will always struggle with time management. It is not a good management style.

b.   Learn how to communicate with people effectively. Everyone has a primary behavioural style and a primary learning modality. When you learn to communicate with someone based on their primary behaviour style and learning modality, the communication is significantly more effective, saving you enormous amounts of time.

As you can see, learning how to create better time management skills is not a one day event. Gaining the base knowledge in each of these 4 areas can be done quickly. Actually building a thorough knowledge and turning them into valuable skills takes much longer.

The way to implement the development of your time management skills, is to include into your goals and activity planning, a plan to develop the skills in the Self-Discipline and People Management Skills areas.

GOAL SETTING AND PLANNING FORMULA

Having **GREAT** success in business and life is done by having **CLARITY** in the **VISION** of how you want your business and life to be, identifying the key **GOALS** that will help you achieve that vision, putting an action **PLAN** into place and taking continued **ACTION** towards achieving those goals.

> " *You will never get control of your business or life if you don't get control of your time* "
>
> *Peter Johnson*

Over the years of coaching business owners and managing teams, the one thing I notice is that when you start talking about how the way to success is through setting goals and then setting a plan to achieve them, you see most people's eyes roll as they think, ***"I have done all of that and it doesn't work."*** Considering the way it is normally done, I totally agree with them. For most people it doesn't work. I know that I can set a whole list of goals, put a fantastic plan in place aimed at achieving them and get nowhere. You see, I believe we set too many goals, give ourselves too much to do and then get disappointed when we don't achieve anything "within the first week," because we have not had the time to develop our time management skills. We then put the goals in the drawer and that's the last we see of them.

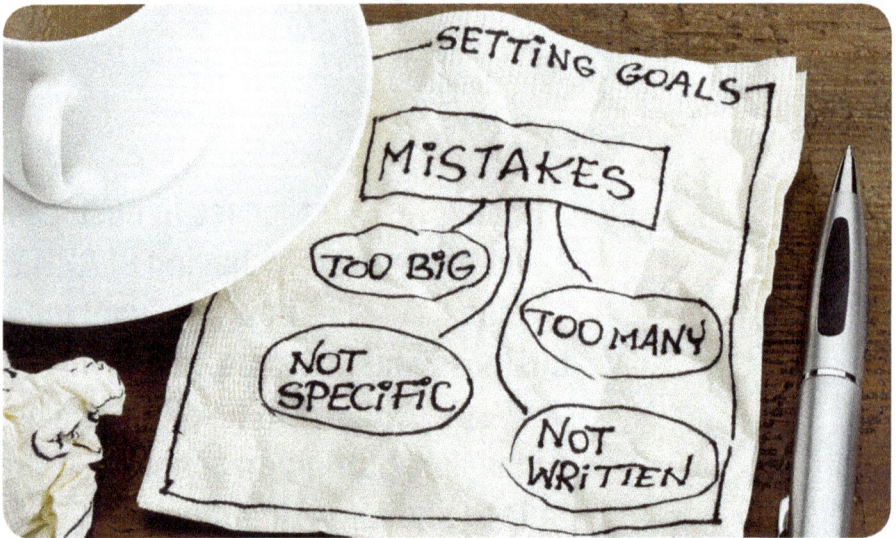

Interestingly enough, if you were to take out that list of goals that you put in the drawer, you will more than likely find that as you read down the list, you will actually tick off a lot of the goals as being achieved, even though you didn't purposely focus on them. This is because the process of writing down the goals and reading them helps your brain to get a clearer picture of what you want and your Reticular Activating System (RAS) sets the brain's compass towards achieving them without you being fully conscious of it. 80% of people learn through visual (physically seeing) or kinaesthetic (touching, feeling things) learning modalities. So the practice of writing (kinaesthetic) and then reading (visual) etches the goal into your subconscious to a far greater extent than just thinking about it does and therefore increases your chances of achieving it.

THE TIME RETRIEVER
Goal Setting and Planning Formula

The formula is based around identifying the **3 key things you need to achieve over a set period (generally 12 months)** that will create the success you are looking for. It is a well-known fact that if you take the time to identify what the goal is, what needs to be done and how you are going to do it, it gets done more quickly and with a far better result than you had anticipated. So even though you say, "*I don't have the time to plan because I'm just too busy,*" you are fooling yourself.

> **If you don't get control of your time, you won't get control of your business or life.**

Most people are too busy doing things in their business and are getting very little forward movement because they don't really know what they want to achieve. When you put together a list of the goals you would like to achieve over 12 months and then identify **Your 3 Key Goals** on that list, you give yourself a significantly greater chance of succeeding. Give yourself a break; it is much easier to focus on 3 goals than 10, 20, 25 or more goals. When you identify Your 3 Key Goals, you will notice that other goals on the list are actually steps that need to be completed on the way to achieving one of Your 3 Key Goals.

By determining the time frame in which you plan to achieve each goal, you can then set up your annual and quarterly planners, which will focus on what various activities need to be completed and when, to achieve the goals. We then use our diary to plan the weekly and daily activities.

As you fine-tune your skills of planning and taking action, you will then be able to determine one key factor in the whole process. That is identifying your Key Focus Point. The Key Focus Point is the one thing that you can identify that if you focus on and carry out every day, your success is guaranteed. A couple of weeks ago, I was talking to a colleague in Sydney about what we were doing with marketing in our businesses, when he made a specific statement: ***"The key is, what I need to focus on is contacting 3 prospects a day and doing 5 online presentations each week and I know I will achieve my targets."*** That is a Key Focus Point.

When it comes to the crunch, it comes down to how much money you bring in. If you generate the revenue that you plan for, then you can be reasonably assured that everything else will fall into place. This means that one of Your 3 Key Goals has to be a revenue figure and the Key Focus Point has to be to something to do with revenue generation. As an example, at Time Retrievers, our Key Focus Point is to have one business commit to being involved in a group coaching program per business day. If this happens, our goals will all be achieved.

THE STEPS IN THE SYSTEM ARE:

1 Determine your Why. Clearly understanding why you are doing what you do and understanding why you are creating your goals and action plan. (Finding Your Why Template)

2 Write down the Vision of what you want your life to be. (Vision Statements Template)

a If you have a business, you will also write down the vision of what your business will look like when it is finished. (Vision Statements Template)

3 List the dreams (Goals) you have. (Goals List)

4 Identify your Personal & Business Goals, required to realise your Vision and Goals. (Goals Planner)

5 Set a time frame for when these goals will be achieved. (Goals Planner)

6 Select the 3 Key Goals that you intend to achieve over the next 12 months. (3 Key Goals Planner)

7 Determine what needs to be done to achieve the 3 Key Goals. (3 Key Goals Planner)

8 Set up the annual plan (12 Month Key Goals Template)

9 Set up the Quarterly Plan (Quarterly Action Plan Template)

10 Weekly planning (Your Diary)

11 Daily planning (Your Diary/To Do List)

12 Determine your Key Focus Point (Quarterly Action Plan Template)

13 Continued actioning of your plan

SYSTEM TEMPLATES:

1. **Finding Your Why Template**

2. **Vision Statements Template**

3. **Goals List**

4. **Lifetime Personal and Business 3 Key Goals Planner**

5. **12 Month Key Goals Planner**

6. **Quarterly Action Plan**

7. **To Do List**

8. **Daily Planning Checklist**

TIP

The best way to work through this program is to read each step, carry out the activity and then move on to the next step. You will build your plan as you go through the book.

STEP ONE

YOUR WHY

When You Understand Your True Why, Focus And Success Is Assured

Your true Why comes from deep within; it will be what you are truly passionate about doing. To find out your true Why, you will need to ask yourself some deep questions about what you really would like to do and achieve in life. Each time you ask the question to yourself, you will come up with an answer. From that answer you continue to ask yourself more questions until you get down to what you are really passionate about.

I have seen some great videos on YouTube and Vimeo that will help you understand the Why process, and in our tools area the Your Why template also has some great questions you can ask yourself as you discover Your Why.

Don't be afraid to have your partner or someone else go through these questions with you, as this will help you get to the root of your passion.

STEP TWO >

YOUR VISION

Have a vision of what your business or life will look like

A Personal Vision is simply the picture you have in your head of what you would love your life to be like. It could be that you simply want to be wealthy and travel all the time, you might like to work for charities full time, you might like to be focused on supporting your family, their children, etc. It might be a mix of things that you would like to do. You ask yourself the question: *"If time and money was not an issue in my life, what would my life be like?"* Then write down all of the things that you can see yourself doing.

A Business Vision is the picture you have in your mind of how you see your business when it is running successfully. Things like what the revenue is, what profit you are making, what products and/or services you are providing, where the business is located, how many locations you are in, how many team members you have and other items you may see. List these items from your mind on to paper, and then write a paragraph on your Vision containing each of these items. Continue to refine your Vision Statement. When developing your Vision, set a time frame for when this Vision will be achieved – 2, 3, 5 years. It's up to you.

Putting your Vision into a written format allows you to clearly understand what you want to achieve and then focus on what to do to achieve it. You will be amazed how you will be clearer about what you need to do when your Vision is on paper.

Sample Vision statement:

Personal

My life is about supporting my family, helping with the grandchildren, being involved in the local Rotary Club, helping to raise funds to support the community locally, Australia-wide and internationally. I want to enjoy playing golf each week and having a date night with my wife each week.

Business

Time Retrievers develops the knowledge, skill and expertise of business owners, assisting them to successfully run their businesses through Group Coaching, 1 to 1 Coaching, specialty business skills development and planning workshops. It has an office/training centre based in Peregian Beach, on the Queensland Sunshine Coast and travels intra- and interstate and worldwide to provide these training services. The team consists of 4 coaches, a workshop co-ordinator and office support personnel.

STEP THREE

SET YOUR GOALS – WHAT DO I WANT TO ACHIEVE?

Determine what you need to accomplish to achieve the vision

Take the time to write a list of what you would like to achieve or do in your life and in your business. This list will need to include items that will need to be successfully completed for you to fulfil your Vision. Remember, this can take a bit of time to do. Once you have written down all of the things you can immediately think of, you will then start to think of the goals that you would like to achieve that are deeper in your feelings. As you carry out this task, think on the basis that time and money are not an issue. *"If I had all of the money and time that I want, what would I do?"* Based on the belief that we should work to live (not live to work), our personal goals will be the driver for what we want to achieve in our business and our life.

This is a perpetual list, also known as a bucket list. Whenever you think of a new goal you would like to achieve, add it to this list. Here are some thought provoking ideas:

Where will I be living... Surfers Paradise, Hawaii, Philip Island, Tampa, Toorak, Townsville

Houses ... How many ... where ... worth ... each one - # beds/baths, other rooms, views, outside, fixtures and fittings

Cars ... make, model, year, colour, interior type and colour

Boats ... make, model, feet, colour, interior, # berths, names, year, jet skis

Bikes ... push, motor, road, dirt, rego plates, colour

Jewellery ... his/hers, watches (make, model, metal/colour stones), necklaces (metal/colour, stones, weight), rings (metal/colour, stones, weight), bracelets and bangles (metal/colour, stones, weight)

Furniture, antique, specially designed and made, marble, internationally designed.

Electronic Stuff ... stereos, DVDs, VCRs, computers, games, telescopes, kitchen, cameras, toys, phones, tools, motorised tools, garden tools, appliances, TVs, cinemas

Art ... paintings, sculptures, photographs, memorabilia, prints, waterscapes

Pets ... dogs, cats, birds, guard dogs, fish, etc.

Investments ... self-managed super fund

Properties ... residential, # beds/baths, suburbs/areas, wealth wheels, blocks of units, monthly passive, total value per year, etc.

Shares ... options, warrants, futures, equities, managed funds, blue chips, tech/biotech, mining, retail, transport, etc.

Cash ... bank accounts in what countries, how much cash in each

Businesses ... how many, turnover/profits, # employees, # offices/stores, industries, etc.

Major Achievements ... business, family, investing, sports/hobbies

Community Service ... member of a Rotary or Lions club or other organisation

Awards ... which ones, from whom, what for

Donations ... time/money, which charities, functions, amounts

Kids Money ... how much, when, what rules, etc.

Sporting/Special Events ... which ones, where and when ...

Holidays ... where, how many weeks per year, what class of travel

Hobbies ... what, how often, at what level

Health ... diet, vitamins

Fitness ... what exercise, where, how long

Seminars ... how many a year, what subjects

Restaurants ... where, how often, which ones

Shows ... which ones, where, how often

Fun Times ... friends, etc.

When setting these goals, remember to use the SMARTER principle:

SPECIFIC – each goal you set needs to be specific, i.e. 5 day holiday to Fiji 15th September 2010. This goal sets the location, the number of days and the date that you want to go. You could even state the resort you want to holiday at. The key is that when you are clear and specific about what you want, your RAS will go to work subconsciously to assist you in achieving it.

MEASURABLE – a goal needs to be measurable to enable you to clearly understand what you have achieved. If your sales conversion rate is 31% and you set a target of 35%, you now have a clear measurement to work with.

ACHIEVABLE – when setting a goal, you need to believe that you can achieve the goal. If the goal is so large that deep down you feel you won't achieve it, then you won't. If the goal is that big, you will need to break it down into smaller goals that will take you step by step through to achieving the big goal.

REALISTIC – a goal needs to be realistic. When you set the goal, there needs to be a realistic chance of achieving it.

TIME – all goals need to have a time frame set for their achievement. This creates the sense of urgency for completing the activities required to achieve the goal.

EXTENDING – your goals should help grow you personally, they should extend you beyond your current level of knowledge, skill and experience. In other words, take you out of your comfort zone.

REWARD – what is the reward you will give yourself or team members for achieving the goal? All successes should be celebrated, whether big or small.

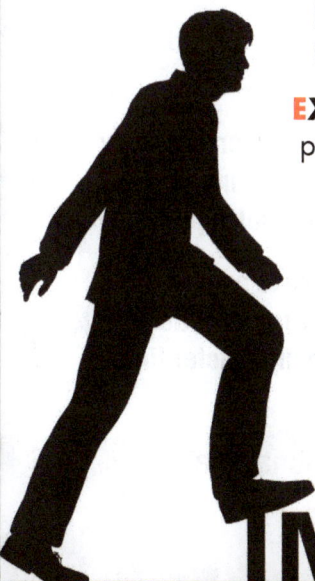

ImPOSSIBLE

BHAG – Big Hairy Audacious Goal

A BHAG is a goal that is so big it is hard to believe you would ever achieve it. This is the ultimate dream, becoming a multi-millionaire, owning a luxury yacht, opening an orphanage in a third world country. These goals are achievable, you just simply have to break them down into what needs to be done over the time frame you set and then get on with achieving each step. Remember how to eat an elephant: one bite at a time. Set your BHAG and go for it.

NEVER FORGET – setting goals is one step, the other is you have to take **ACTION** to achieve them.

BUSINESS TIP

Part of your goal planning needs to include setting a revenue budget for the financial year. Growing your business financially is easier when you know what revenue you intend to achieve. This budget should be broken down into monthly revenue targets.

There are 3 key methods for setting a budget:

1. Using the past year's results, set your budget based on a percentage increase.

2. Use a unit sales forecast. A unit sales forecast is where you look at the item or service you provide, and plan how many of these items/services will be sold each month at their sales price.

3. Set a specific monthly figure that you would like to achieve (this is an easy way to budget, but does not allow for variations in weeks per month, public holidays or traditionally quieter times in the year).

Write these goals down on your Business & Personal Goals Lists.

STEP FOUR

WHEN

Set a time frame for when these goals will be achieved

Set a time frame in years (1, 2, 3, 5, 7, 10 years) when each of these key goals will be achieved. Setting a time frame for when a goal is to be achieved creates a sense of urgency, helps you to stop procrastinating and to get on and do something.

Remember when you got married, were planning a holiday or some other significant event in your life? You set a date and generally a time. Your focus was intense, there was no negotiation. The activities that needed to be planned and carried out absolutely had to be completed by this date and time. There were no exceptions allowed. Go on, take a couple of minutes and think about it, what your thoughts were, what you had to do and how you were determined to make sure everything was done and the event went ahead on time and successfully.

If these goals are really important to you, when you set the date, you will ensure they happen. If not, you need to review these goals and find out what really is important.

SAMPLE

PERSONAL GOALS

3 week holiday in Europe	1 year
Start donating to charities	1 year
Mercedes E 350	3 years
Photography course	1 year
Investment property	2 years
Hybrid bike	1 year
Tour Canada	4 years
Reduce weight to 85kgs	1 year

BUSINESS GOALS

$500,000 revenue	1 year
2nd office	2 years
Work 4 day week	3 years
Relocate premises	1 year
Systemise procedures	1 year
Franchise	4 years
New delivery vehicle	1 year
Sales manager	2 years

Now, go through your goal list and set a time frame for when you expect to achieve them.

Your list of goals should always be available for you to review and to add more goals as they pop up. As you work through your list, you simply mark off each goal as it is achieved.

At least once each year you should sit down and review your whole goal list: reset the target dates, mark off what has been achieved, remove goals that are no longer relevant and then re-sort them so that the next 12 months' goals are at the top of the list.

STEP

FIVE

SEPARATE YOUR NEXT 12 MONTHS' GOALS

We are now at the point where we are going to focus on what we plan to achieve over the next 12 months.

To do this, simply use the **12 Month Key Goals Template** to list all of the goals that you have set to achieve over the next year. *See Page 66.*

STEP SIX

3 KEY GOALS FOR SUCCESS

Select the 3 key goals that will lead to your success

From the list of Personal and Business Goals, review your goals that are to be achieved over the next 12 months and select the 3 Key Goals that you will focus on to gain your success. One goal will be the revenue target, the rest can be a mix of personal and business goals.

To do this, ask yourself, *"If I only achieve one of these goals, which one is the most important one to be achieved?"* Once you have the answer, ask this same question again, to select the 2nd and 3rd Key Goals for the next 12 months.

The remaining goals on the lists are still targeted to be achieved throughout the year. However, our main focus is to ensure that these 3 important goals are achieved as a minimum by year end.

Write these goals onto the 3 Key Goals to Success Planner. See page 64.

Some sample goals could be:

1. Achieve $500,000 business revenue.   5.00pm 30th June 2015

2. Relocate the business to new premises.   31st January 2015

3. 3 week holiday touring Europe.   1st May 2015

STEP SEVEN 〉〉

HOW

Determine what you need to do to achieve the goals

Now that you have determined what goals you need to achieve and when they will be achieved by, you need to determine what actions need to be taken to successfully complete the goals.

List all the activities that need to be carried out to achieve the goals and then place them into the sequence that they need to be carried out in. The revenue goal will have the most primary activities as there will be several steps towards achieving it. The steps in the revenue goal will include the marketing plan which will have its own planning process that is then overlaid into the annual and quarterly plans.

As you determine the steps required to achieve Your 3 Key Goals, you will notice that some of the other goals you listed will actually be smaller steps on the way to achieving Your 3 Key Goals. This means you will actually have success in achieving more of the goals on your original list.

GOAL 1 - ACHIEVE $500,000 IN REVENUE

STEPS

Set budget by month	30/06/2015
Develop marketing plan	30/06/2015
2 sales training sessions each month – 1st session start by	15/07/2015
2 new sales reps: 1 in September, 1 in February	01/09/2015
Sales leadership competition to start	01/01/2015

STEP EIGHT

THE 12 MONTH KEY GOALS PLANNER

Prepare your 12 month key goals planner

The 12 Month Key Goals Planner provides you with a snapshot view of what you intend to do for the year. The 3 Key Goals are shown in the year end result at the top of the planner. In each quarter and month, add the revenue plan and key activities for each period. In the boxes linked to each month, note the main activities for the key goals and other activities from your marketing plan and the significant events.

See the sample 12 Month Key Goals Planner on page 66.

STEP NINE ❯

QUARTERLY ACTION PLAN

Prepare your quarterly action plan

The Quarterly Action Plan is prepared at the beginning of each quarter. It is one of the main focus tools for achieving success. You take each of the goals that are planned to be achieved over the next 3 months and place them into the Quarterly Action Plan in the month that they will be achieved. Then using the **HOW** (Step 7), plan the weekly activities that you will need to carry out to successfully complete the goals.

In the attached sample plan, you will see that there have been key goals set for the quarter; these goals are then broken down into what needs to be achieved each month. In each month, the **HOW** activities (Step 7) are placed into the week that they are intended to be carried out in (each month has 5 boxes, and the date for the start of each week is placed above each weekly box. In months where there are 4 weeks, simply disregard the first box in that month).

See the sample Quarterly Action Plan on page 68.

TIME MANAGEMENT

WEEKLY PLANNING

Planning your week is crucial to making the best use of your time and therefore ensuring you maximise your achievements over the week. Your weekly plan needs to be prepared before the day that starts your week. Most people will plan their week from Monday to Sunday, which means that your weekly plan will be prepared by Sunday evening ready to start on Monday morning. To prepare our plan, we need our diary (whether it is electronic, MS Outlook, etc. or a paper diary system), our Quarterly Action Plan, rolling To Do List and knowledge of events that will be happening in that week.

DEFAULT DIARY:

A Default Diary is the best way to plan your week. Most people will say that they are unable to plan their week as they do so many things. **Getting control of your business and your life is based around getting control of your time.** If you take the time to evaluate what activities you do, you will see that some activities can be grouped together and be carried out on certain days and what activities are wasting your time.

To do this, we need to track our activities for a 2 week period. This process is a bit tedious, but you will be surprised at what information you gain from this exercise and how you can start to free some of your time by combining activities that you do into specific periods of the week.

At the end of the 2 weeks, review the information you have and then determine what activities can be grouped together and carried out at a certain time of the week. Determine which activities can be eliminated from your week, either by having someone else do them or simply by not doing them at all.

The exercise will give you an indication of how you are currently using your time and what changes you need to make to make the best to use of your time.

Print out or photocopy a page from your diary; you will need a blank diary page for each day. As you work through each day, make a note of what you did for each 15 minute period of that day. Put a dollar sign $ next to each activity that directly generated revenue. Review the information from each day, and group together activities that can be planned for specific days or certain times of the day.

Some of the things you will find out are:

1. **Appointments –** instead of setting appointments at sporadic times through the week, create time frames for when you make appointments, e.g. Tuesday mornings 9.00am to 12.00 midday, Wednesdays 1.00pm to 5.00pm, Thursdays 11.00am to 3.00pm. Grouping appointments enables you to make the best use of your time whilst you are out of the office. There are no doubt times when urgent appointments need to be made outside of these times; however, you will find that by giving a range of times during these default periods, most people you are making an appointment with will be able to fit in to these times.

2. **Cold calling telephone calls –** an activity that most people continue to defer and don't do or do poorly. Set aside periods of 1 to 2 hours at specific times on certain days and then as Nike says, "Just Do It." Set a goal for what result you require from each period you make the calls (say 3 appointments) and then when this goal is achieved, move onto the next planned task.

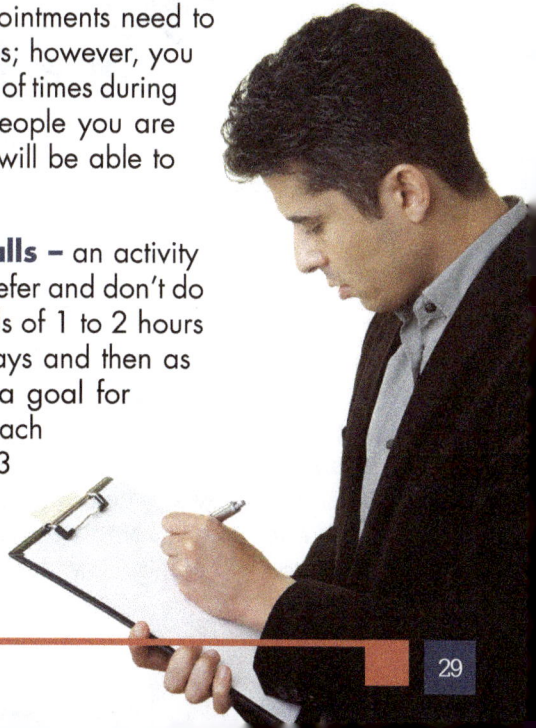

3. **Office tasks –** combine office-based tasks together and allow 2 or 3 periods during the week when they will be done.

4. **Personal development/health –** both of these items are of high importance. Without good health, you cannot properly support your family, business or your life. Development of your knowledge and skills will always take you forward in achieving your business and lifetime ambitions. You need to plan non-negotiable time during the week for these activities to be carried out.

5. **Planning time –** the more you plan and action that plan, the more you will achieve. We need to set aside time to plan our week and each day.

ROLLING TO DO LIST:

A rolling To Do List is a list of activities that you continually update by adding new items as they are required and crossing off activities as you complete them.

As you go though each day, there are always items that come up that you need to action at some point in time. Instead of trying to remember them, I keep separate blank pages in my diary that I just continually add items to that need to be actioned at some point in time. By adding these items to the list, I can review them on a regular basis and ensure that they get done. As each one is completed, it is crossed off the list. This system will eliminate you forgetting to do things.

PLAN YOUR WEEK:

1. To plan your week, open your diary to the week to an opening, and review your appointments that have already been recorded. In your rolling To Do List, look for out of office items that can be carried out before or after these appointments and plan them into your week.

2. Next, look at the activities that are planned in your Quarterly Action Plan. Determine how long each activity will take and then plan these activities into your week by scheduling an appointment time on the most appropriate day. You have determined that these activities are crucial to the success of your plan and for you to achieve your goals, so you need to ensure that you treat these appointments as you would any other appointment. Activities from your Quarterly Action Plan should also appear in your daily To Do List as an A-graded activity.

3. Once you have completed steps 1 & 2, you then need to plan in other activities that you intend to do during the week. Don't try to plan every minute of your week – leave time for unplanned activities to be carried out as well.

TIP

Look at the bookends of your week – Monday morning, Friday afternoon. What do you do during these time frames? Wind up your week and wind down your week?

Without good planning, poor use of these time frames wastes 20% of your week (that's one whole day).
You could set appointments during these times and make full use of the week.

STEP ELEVEN

PLANNING YOUR DAY

The key to achieving is to plan what you want to achieve. It does not have to be an elaborate plan, just a plan that allows you to clearly understand what you expect to achieve, what needs to be done and how you are going to do it. Some people like to make their plan exactly perfect before they start doing it, and don't get it done. If this is you, when the plan is 80% done get on with making it happen – the rest will fall into place as you go.

I have heard people say that when they plan their day with a To Do List, they didn't get anything on the list done and that it was a waste of time. Well, at least you knew what had not been done and if you kept the list would not forget to do the important activities (which is what usually happens). On the other hand, you will have days when you get all of the activities on the list done by lunchtime. The simple fact is that, if you plan what you need to do to achieve your goals, you will get a lot more done and actually achieve your goals. **However, don't forget, you have to take action to make it all work.**

Have you ever experienced waking up at 2.00am, 3.15am, or 4.30am with your mind going at a million miles an hour thinking of things you need to do? You found it hard to get back to sleep because your mind is continually working. This may even happen several times in a night and then you wake up in the morning tired because your sleep was interrupted and then when you go to write down what your mind was thinking about, you can't remember it. Very frustrating.

The simple way to reduce the amount of times this happens is to plan your day the night before. By planning the night before, you enable your subconscious to work on ways to get the activities on your plan completed without disturbing your sleep. When you are in control by having a plan, your mind is settled, when you do not have a plan your mind is set into alarm mode trying to keep track of what you need to do, thus stimulating the brain and waking you up.

I find that when I plan the night before, I do not wake up during the night thinking about what needs to be done. And yet if I haven't planned the next day, my sleep is disturbed by thoughts of what I need to do.

To plan your day, you need the following items:

1. **Diary**
2. **Your rolling To Do List**
3. **Your weekly diary plan**
4. **Your Quarterly Action Plan**
5. **Knowledge of events and activities that are on during that week**

In preparing your day, you need to review the appointments that are already set in your diary and activities from your Quarterly Action Plan that you have already placed into that day. List any items that are on your rolling To Do List that you need to do on that day.

We now need to prioritise the list based on the level of importance of each item. Using the A B C method, each activity is given a rating based on their level of importance. A – must be done today; B – needs to be done; C – do if time available. Items from your Quarterly Action Plan must be rated as an A.

Once this rating is done, you need to number the items in relation to their priority of being done: A1, A2, A3, B1, B2, B3, C1, C2. Next we need to review the plan to ensure that we have covered what we need to do tomorrow. It should take no more than 30 minutes to plan your day.

Eat That Frog – you may be familiar with Brian Tracy's book *Eat That Frog*. This book focuses on the fact that most people tend to put off doing hard or difficult activities in favour of completing quick and easy tasks. The general problem is that the difficult or hard activity is generally the most important activity that needs to be done. Think back to when there was an activity you needed to do, but you kept putting it off and did other easier activities.

At some point in time, you still had to do it. By putting it off, it kept playing on your mind, and generally raised your stress levels and made you less effective. It may have been making telephone cold calls, dismissing or retrenching an employee, counselling a poorly performing employee, ringing an angry customer, or something that was going to take so long to do that you decided to do the other easier tasks first. Think about the stress and constant drain on your energy that went on until you carried out the task. When you finally carried the task out, it all went and you were able to get on with it.

When you plan your day, you need to make sure you Eat That Frog first. If the difficult or time-consuming task is the A1 most important task, then it should be done first. Once it is completed, you will have a clear mind and be able to give 100% focus to the next priority item. You will be able to get on and do the easier activities and will also be on your way to achieving the key goals you have set.

In setting our Daily Plan, we need to combine the set appointments with the To Do items. Where there is an appointment set that is Out of The Office, we should also include other out of office activities to be carried out before or after that activity whilst we are out on the road. The plan of To Do items should start with the A1 task and work though all the As then Bs and Cs. At the end of the day, the items not completed are then assessed with the To Do items for the next day and planned in based on their re-assessed priority with the next day's activities.

Template – Daily Planning Checklist - See page 79.

TIP

Plan to do activities that are based on achieving success in the future first. Most people plan to do activities that are related to what is happening right now first and then plan to do activities that are aimed at achieving future success after that.

STEP TWELVE

KEY FOCUS POINT

Find a specific action that if done daily will guarantee you success

Finding your Key Focus Point will not happen immediately. You will need to spend some time working with your plans to clearly identify what it is that if you achieved it on a daily basis, you would achieve your goals. As stated earlier, achieving your financial goals is the key to succeeding with most of your goals. With this is mind, the Key Focus Point needs to be an activity that generates income and needs to be results orientated.

Some example focus points are:

- 1 x sale per day at your planned average dollar sale
- 1 business committing to a workshop per day
- 2 number of new customers per day
- 1 customer upgrade per day

STEP THIRTEEN

CONTINUED ACTION

Now that you have set your plan, you need to commit to taking continuous action towards success

Now comes the most important part. You have done all of the work determining what you want to achieve and how you are going to achieve it. We are at the point where most people create failure in their plan. They simply don't take the continuous action that is necessary to make the plan a reality. We come back to the old "I just got too busy and didn't have the time to do it." I thought you wanted success, so it's up to you – you are the one who must make it happen day in day out.

Plans should not be set in concrete. However, when we set our Quarterly Action Plan, we need to be committed to making it happen. New ideas should not be added during the quarter unless totally necessary. They should be added to the list of items to be reviewed in your next Quarterly Action Plan. If you keep changing your plan daily, weekly or monthly, you will start running around directionless and will not achieve your goals.

GOALS

Mission

Vision

Values

PART 2

WHAT STOPS YOU FROM FOCUSING ON AND ACHIEVING YOUR GOALS?

CREATING THE SUCCESS HABIT

Building your list of goals and creating an action plan may take some time to do. However, the hardest part is staying focused on the goals, sticking to your action plan and carrying out the activities that you have determined are required to create the success over the long term. Very few people are able to stick to their plan of action beyond the first 2 weeks. If it is new to you or you have been trying time and time again, you need to be aware that you are now looking to change your thought patterns, your habits and your beliefs in order to create the habit of success.

To help you understand why you need to push yourself to stay focused on reviewing your plan and carrying out the actions in your plan on a daily basis and developing the new thought patterns, new habits and new beliefs of setting goals, creating action plans and sticking to them, I found this item in a blog by Andrea Pettit from her *Right From the Heart* website (15th October 2010). I have also heard Jack Canfield and John Assaraf talk about this study.

Changing your Non-conscious Brain

As my posts have been describing our non-conscious brains are extremely powerful. They are where our habits are created and stored. This is where self-limiting beliefs are created and stored. I first heard of this from Jack Canfield and then again from John Assaraf. They both describe a study done by NASA. NASA made astronauts in training wear a set of glasses that turned the world around them upside down. They were made to wear these glasses for 24 hours a day, 7 days a week. What they found surprised them at the time. They found that after 21–30 days the astronauts that wore these glasses continuously suddenly had a switch. Apparently, their brains automatically flipped their world back. Their brains were trained to turn the world back around right side up even though they were wearing these glasses. They also found that if anyone removed the glasses before this 21–30 day interval, they would have to start completely over and go through another 21–30 day interval to have this phenomenon occur.

John Assaraf spent time finding out why this happened and what he found out was that our brains have a RAS (Reticular Activating System). This is basically a way for our brains to create pathways. These pathways become the non-conscious beliefs (empowering or self-limiting) and the habits (good and bad) that we create. By working with this system we can change the self-limiting beliefs and habits that we want to.

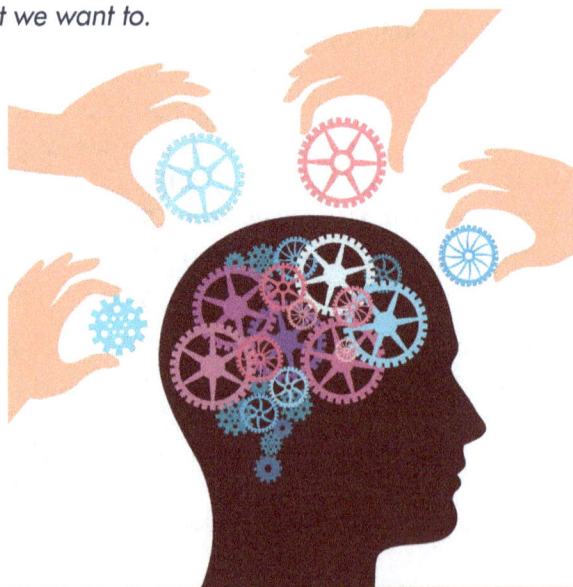

2.1 Procrastination

Procrastination is one of the 3 big road blocks for starting to get control of your time. We build our plans and are excited to start implementing them, only to find that we start procrastinating and start to avoid doing the activities that we have planned to do.

Is this familiar to you?

- **We put off tasks that will take some time to do**
    - We say to ourselves, *"I know it's number one on my list for today, but I will get this done and that done etc., etc., and then get onto it"* – only to find it doesn't get done.

- **We put off tasks that are difficult to do**
    - Again, we say to ourselves, *"I know it's number one on my list for today, but I will get this done and that done etc., etc., and then get onto it"* – only to find it doesn't get done.

- **We put off doing things we don't like doing**
    - Inside, our thoughts are telling us we don't like doing this, so we say to ourselves, *"I'll do it this afternoon,"* then in the afternoon, we say to ourselves, *"it's OK, I don't need to have it done until tomorrow, so I'll do it in the morning"* – and it goes on and on.

- **We put off difficult conversations**
    - If we need to confront someone, have a performance discussion with an employee or need to terminate an employee, we find ourselves putting off these discussions, often by telling ourselves this will be a better time to do it.

- **We often put off decisions that involve money**
    - This is generally because we don't have a clear plan of how to handle our finances.

The best way to eliminate these 5 reasons for avoiding things is to have a **Do It Now Mentality**.

The major issue here is how we think — it is about what has happened in our past that has created our current thoughts, beliefs, habits and patterns. Over time, you meet so many people who live in their past, who struggle to have a great future because they simply can't let go of the past.

It is important to use your past as an education for your future, not an anchor. Research has shown that the average person has 40,000 to 60,000 thoughts per day. If your thoughts are negative, you will feel down, tired, "I can't do that," "it never works for me," "they will just screw me over again."

The key thing about human beings is our ability to choose our thoughts. As an example, if you are feeling negative about your finances, you know the old, "I don't know how I'm going to pay the bills," "if I go to the letter box, it will only be more bills that I can't pay," "whatever I do, it doesn't work for me." You need to change your focus to "what am I doing right now to generate the income I need?" and "what is the best use of my time right now?" These types of questions will serve your future much better.

> "We are what we think. All that we are arises with our thoughts. With our thoughts, we make the world"
>
> - The Buddha

> "The greatest weapon against stress is our ability to choose one thought over another"
>
> - William James

You notice each of those positive statements I talked about right now. That is because the present moment is the only time you can actually do anything for your future, so it is important to not be focused on the negative, but to focus on what you can do to go forward right now.

You plan for the future, your past is the education, and the present moment is for doing the activities that will create your positive future.

DISCIPLINE

Discipline is the ability to do something even though every part of you wants to do something else that is more fun or easy to do. Successful people have the ability to discipline themselves to do the things that they have to do to achieve what they want to achieve. You need to be the same.

I am a spontaneous person. I spent years in service management where I believe my skills were most suited as I had the ability to think quickly under the fire of many issues at one time, create a plan of action and get all the issues resolved. I played in Quadrant 1 of Stephen Covey's Time Management Matrix.

I spent years setting goals and building plans that I did not have the discipline to continually work on. At the end of the month, quarter or year, I was nowhere near on track. The plans were right there in front of me, but I hadn't been able to stick with them. I always thought that it was just my make-up – I am good at responding to the urgent, but not good at working to my plan and creating long-term results. From working with people over the years, I believe a great percentage of you believe the same about yourselves. You have to discipline yourself to create the habits necessary to achieve your goals.

DETERMINATION

There has to be a determination within you to stay on track and achieve your goals. The best way I can get you to understand determination is for you to think back in time to an event you were planning that really had your focus. Two types of events that most people have enormous focus and determination for are their weddings or big holidays. When I run workshops or speak at events, I ask the participants to think back to one of these events, how they felt about it, what the feeling was inside them, the intensity to have it planned well and for everything to happen as planned and at the time it was planned. In these events everything has to be planned and organised well in advance of the event, and on the day everything has to happen on time – there is no leeway for slipping the time back one or two hours or even a day or so.

Some would prefer not to think back to it, as it may not have turned out well in the long run. But they do see how focused they were, the determination to ensure everything was right and on time and how over the months and sometimes years before the event, they were constantly working on their plan towards the event. You need to apply this same focus and determination to your important life and business goals.

PAYING THE PRICE

To achieve something at a high level, you have to, as the saying goes "Be Prepared To Pay The Price." If you want to be an Olympian, top level football player, dancer, doctor, lawyer, etc., you have to be prepared to give up doing what everyday people do and focus on your chosen career. Getting up early to train, training late, having very little social life, pushing yourself hard and studying long hours are just some of what these people do to become top of their game. They don't go out every Friday and Saturday night to the clubs with their friends, or sleep in until midday – they are totally focused on doing what it takes to be Number 1.

To become consistent at achieving your goals, you don't have to go to the extremes of athletes, etc. (you can if you want to) but you must still be prepared to pay the price. That price is doing whatever it takes to make you create the habit of reviewing your goals each day and following your plan, and carrying out the activities designed to achieve those goals on a daily basis. This is a day-to-day focus, you commit to doing it and then work on making yourself do it each day. As the NASA study showed, if you can do it for 21 to 30 consecutive days, you will start to create new pathways in your brain and form the habit that will lead you to success. Miss one day, and the 21 to 30 day period starts over again.

So it's not just the process of setting goals and creating action plans that will lead to you achieving what you want to achieve, it is having the discipline and determination, and being prepared to pay the price of whatever it takes that will create your success.

You have created your success program using the Time Retriever tools. Now decide what you will do to keep you on track on a daily basis. Set alarms on your clock, calendar, phone, have your phone provider give you a reminder call each day, have a friend or family member call you each day, just simply decide what you will put in place to keep you focused and on track.

2.2 Distractions & Interruptions

Business Owners/Managers with Team Members

Over many years, I have worked with business owners and managers of small, medium and large businesses who tell me that they have tried the process of setting goals, creating To Do Lists and planning their day, but it all falls into a heap when they arrive at the office. Even for those that have been to time management courses or workshops and have done everything that they were taught, it still doesn't work.

That is because a vital part was left out: they are managers of people. In their goal setting and planning process, did they ask themselves, "**When I am working my day, what are the things that will stop me from completing my plan?**" Generally the answers will be interruptions from team members, phone calls, crisis management, etc. The key is that you will need to drill down further with this question, asking yourself, "**what creates this situation?**" Answers will be: team members that don't make decisions themselves, customers that will only deal with you, a sales team that can't sell, systems that don't work or are not in place, the wrong team members on the payroll and many more.

All of these answers come back to one key issue – your management skills. You may be excellent at managing your time, but your skills of managing your team and your business may need to be developed further. The simple fact is that these skills will always be in continuous development, and will always have an effect on managing your time.

Here are some key areas in business that will have a hidden effect on your ability to achieve your action plan:

1. **Marketing** – it doesn't matter whether you manage just yourself or a team of thousands, understanding the fundamentals of marketing and keeping up-to-date with current trends will always enable you to develop and action a good marketing plan, or question a marketing plan that has been put forward to you. Just accepting a plan because someone has marketing qualifications is not

acceptable. There are plenty of people out there with marketing qualifications who will never generate income for a company. Being trained in the fundamentals of marketing will ensure you make the best use of your marketing time.

2. **Sales** – without sales, you have no business, so it makes sense that you ensure that you are continually developing your sales and sales management skills. I have worked with quite a few sales representatives and sales teams over the years, and have always noticed that the good sales representatives are always developing their sales skills, which helps them utilise their time more productively. A lot of your time and your sales team's time can be lost through poor sales skills.

3. **Recruiting** – this is one of the key areas where business owners and managers lose a lot of time and money. Knowing the correct methods of recruiting people into your business is critical to the success of your business. Through a good training course, you will have a clear understanding of why following a solid recruitment process will help you build good skills in recruiting the right people into your business, resulting in you being able to manage your time more effectively.

4. **Leading your team** – as your business grows, your responsibility to the business will focus more and more on managing the team and the strategic direction of the company. A critical element of this is continually developing your leadership skills. This is not a case of just going and doing a leadership course and then that's it – this development is a lifetime process. The key is that you need to have something in your plans that has you sourcing the development of your skills.

Having worked in and with various sized businesses over the years, the management of the team has been the most difficult part of running a business. There is always some sort of issue that comes up that you have to deal with, which results in your planning of your day being totally shot to pieces. Although you will always come across new issues that can be difficult, constantly developing your leadership and people management skills will help you deal with these issues and your time more effectively.

5. **Creating sustainability in your business** – as the owner or manager of a business, your role is to ensure that systems and processes are put into place aimed at ensuring the business's future success with the least amount of resource. This means that you are responsible for planning the future direction of the business and ensuring that the business has effective systems and processes in place that, combined with the latest technology, enable the marketing, sales, recruiting and leadership areas to operate at their maximum capability.

Through the implementation of these systems and processes, your team will have a clear understanding of what they are required to do and how they do it. This in turn results in less interruption to your day, and therefore greater control over your management of your time. A clear example of sustainable systems and processes in business is the McDonald's system. They work on the basis that everything in the business has a clearly defined process to follow, and when followed correctly the business operates very effectively.

6. **Your business will not make you wealthy** – this is a lesson I learnt from Brad Sugars: *"Your business will not make you wealthy, investing your profits into quality investments will create your wealth."* The ultimate in time management is to be in a position that when you get out of bed each day, you choose whether you want to work or play. Your role in your business is to generate a profit that you can invest, and from those investments you gain an ongoing income.

You will no doubt have seen businesses where as they become successful, the owners start to buy the expensive cars, boats, holiday homes, etc., using the money directly earned by the business. You may also have seen businesses go bust and all of these luxuries disappear. This may have happened to you. Using Brad's formula, the money from the business is invested into quality investments and the returns from these investments are what you use to buy the luxury items. This will ensure that you can have them forever.

A great quote I heard from, I believe it was Michael Angiers at www.successnet.org, is *"Your responsibility is to ensure you create an impregnable financial barrier around your family."* Through achieving this result, you will also have control of your time management.

ELIMINATING INTERRUPTIONS

As a business owner or manager, the planning process for setting your goals and action plan needs to include the question, *"what are the things that will interrupt my ability to focus on completing my highest priority activities each day?"* Then include in those goals and your action plan items aimed at eliminating these interruptions.

To identify these interruptions, you will need to keep track of what the distractions are. Create yourself a form, or use The Time Retriever Distraction Buster Tool in the back of this book to track your interruptions.

The process is:

1. **On the Distraction Buster Tool, write down the details of each interruption you experience during the day.**

   When doing this you will need to note the following:

   a. **Time of interruption** – enables you to see if there is a time pattern in the interruption

   b. **Who or what it was that interrupted you**

   c. **What the details of the interruption were**

   d. **Create a code system to identify specific types of interruption**
      i. C – Customer
      ii. S – Sales skills
      iii. P – Product knowledge
      iv. F – Finances
      v. Pe – Personal
      vi. A – Administration
      vii. Sy – System issues
      viii. W – Warehousing
      ix. L – Lack of concentration
      x. X – My Headspace/Motivation

2. **After 2 weeks, review the data and create a list of the key reasons you are interrupted during the day.**

3. **Prioritise the list, starting with the item that interrupts you the most, to the item that interrupts you the least.**

4. **Starting with Number 1, determine what needs to be done to eliminate the interruption.**

5. **Create your plan for eliminating this interruption and include it in your quarterly, weekly and daily planning process.**

When I started using this process many years ago, I was able to discover exactly what distracted me from being able to manage my time more effectively and was able to create the plans and actions required to eliminate them over time. This gained me back hours in my day.

One example of what I found:

I had a sales rep who constantly interrupted my day to ask questions about a series of typewriter models and the servicing of those typewriters. I was not aware of how much he interrupted me until I tracked the interruptions in my day.

Once it became obvious to me, I looked at what the problem was, and found that he had not been fully trained on how to sell the typewriter and how we service it. I arranged for him to be trained on the typewriters' capabilities and our servicing process over a 2 week period with a product specialist, and he rarely interrupted me again. What I did receive from him was a very gracious thank you gift, as he was now selling more typewriters than he had ever sold before.

Over the years I have seen this happening with business owners who have to have complete control over everything. They do not provide the necessary information to their team that would allow them to get on with their day and do their job properly. They also do not allow their team to make decisions, requiring them to come to the owner for everything. I know I have heard all of the reasons for this, but the simple fact is, whilst they continue to do this, they also continue to say, "*there are never enough hours in the day.*" Successful people don't do this.

If you take the time to implement and follow this process, you will be amazed how much time you get back in your day.

2.3 Time Tips

Business Mums/Dads

When you decide to become a Business Mum/Dad (I have included Business Dads here, because although I have not personally met a Dad who is a stay at home Dad looking after the children and starting a business, there is or will be stay at home Dads who do) there are some key items you will need to understand to ensure you achieve success in your business.

Know how much time you really have to work on your business. I have worked with quite a number of Business Mums over the years, and the biggest issue is getting them to clearly understand how much time they really have to run their business. When you get them to prepare a weekly default diary, most are shocked to see that they only have around 3½ hours of productive time available during the business day, and they also use around 1 hour in the evening. Some have a few hours on the weekend. These available times can vary from business to business, with some having even less time.

The issue is that they measure themselves against businesses and people who have a full-time focus and set their expectations around this measurement. Once we are able to establish what time they have available, we have been able to set sensible goals and action plans that enable them to be successful in their business. For most Business Mums/Dads, their dream is to generate an income whilst at the same time they are home and available for their children and partners when needed.

Some key points for Business Mums/Dads are:

1. You still need to create your business plan, set your goals and targets and create an action plan aimed at achieving these goals. You need to remember the SMARTER principles for goal setting to ensure you set goals that fit with the time frame you have available.

2. For children under school age, try to have an arrangement where someone trustworthy – grandparent, good friend, or crèche – is able to look after them for your defined number of hours each week, to enable you to attend appointments and more importantly have some focused time to work on important tasks.

3. Coffee catch-up with friends, etc. – you still need to associate with friends and other people. Arrange these coffee catch-ups either at your lunch break time or if you have to pick up the children from school, arrange the coffee catch-up for the 30 to 45 minutes prior to the pick-up time. Don't do 2 trips.

4. If you have older children, have them help you with activities that they can do. They can earn some pocket money and learn to understand the value of work and income.

5. Don't lose sight of why you started the business in the first place. I have seen Mums start their business, start becoming quite busy as the business builds its success, and then strike problems with family and other issues which makes everything fall into a heap. Know Your Why and build around it.

6. Business Mums/Dads have the ability to build a real business due to necessity. Because you have limited time available, as your business grows, you will need to use the services of other people. This needs to be thought about before you get your business underway as it can become an issue quite quickly. We recommend that you build your business with the focus on you managing the growth and development of the business and employ/contract other people to do the actual work. This will make the best use of your time and you will always have the flexibility to cope with those interruptions to your business routine, with minimal effect on the business's ability to service your customers, as your team will be carrying out the work. We have had several Business Mums achieve this result.

7. Is your business a hobby or a business? If you want it to be a business, treat and manage it like a business.

8. Networking is an important part of business – ensure that you have a clear plan for attending networking events, and don't go to events trying to sell your product or service – go to build relationships for long term business. Only attend events that are of real value for the time you have available to put into attending.

9. Stick to your plan – using the Time Retriever system, you will create a Quarterly Action Plan as you enter each quarter of the year. One of the issues I see with Business Mums is that because they are generally very sociable, they will be attending all sort of groups and getting all sorts of ideas from a wide range of people. They then want to implement all of these ideas immediately and never give any idea enough chance to work.

If you look at the traits of highly successful people, you will see that they put a plan into place and work that plan until it either works or fails. They don't chop and change their plans every second week. You have to give your strategies a chance to work – the new idea might sound great, but you need to put it on the ideas list for review when you do your next Quarterly Action Plan. Everyone thinks they have to do it now or they will miss out. That is rubbish – you will miss out because you keep changing your strategies.

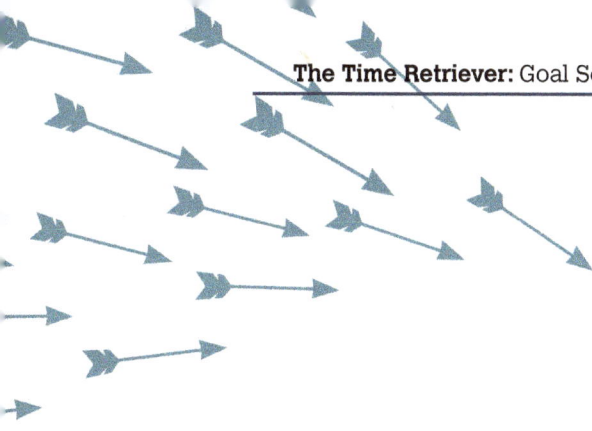

2.4 How to Focus on Your Goals and Action Plans

Now you have set your goals and created the first Quarter's Action Plan, you will need to create your system for reviewing your goals and actions on a daily basis. Remember, if creating a daily To Do List and reviewing your goals is not something you already do on a daily basis, you will need to work hard at creating this habit. You will recall the NASA study – it took 21 to 30 days continuous wearing of the glasses before the brain turned the image back to its normal state.

Create your daily system – in Planning Your Day (Step 11), it was recommended that you plan your day the night before. Set a specific time at the end of your day when you will take the time to review your currents day's results, review your active projects and goals, and then create your prioritised list of actions for tomorrow. To help you create this habit, you can set audible alarms on your clocks, phones, computer, etc. You could ask your partner or someone to remind you, asking, "*have you planned tomorrow yet?*" Just create some sort of system that will make it happen.

This is where the whole process can start to fall apart – you miss one day and you are back at day one in forming the habit. If the time comes and you are not in a position to do the planning, reset the timer on your clock, phone, etc., to a time later in the evening when time will be available. If you know earlier in the day that you won't be able to do it at the normal time or later, do the planning earlier in the day.

Create a checklist of things you need to check whilst you are planning tomorrow – things like check your weekly plan, check your To Do list, check with your partner what's in their plan for tomorrow, check the projects you are working on. This helps you to ensure that you cover everything that may affect the next day. This may look time-consuming, but once you have a system in place, it generally only takes about 10 to 15 minutes to plan your day.

Hour of Power – there are several versions of the Hour of Power. In a time management system, the Hour of Power is about creating time to focus on an important task. In the Hour of Power method, you set aside 60 or 90 minutes of time when you are not disturbed by anyone or anything. You let your team know that you are not to be disturbed, you do not take any phone calls from the office phone or mobile, you close your email system and put your mobile phone away so you are not distracted by SMS messages or anything else.

Now you have secluded yourself, you focus on getting your most important action activity completed or doing the part of the activity that you can do on that day. These items will be the ones that at present your keep saying to yourself, "*I just can't get the time to do them.*"

There were two things I used to do if I was struggling to achieve this uninterrupted time whilst I was in my office. One was to go to the local library for the 60 to 90 minutes and do the work there. The other was that when I booked my car in for a service, I would tell the mechanic that I was going to wait around for the car to be serviced, and asked them to give me a call when it was ready. I would then go to a local coffee shop and work on the important items that I needed to do. It also ensured that my car was serviced quickly.

2.5 Tools To Use

Most people find it hard to stay focused on achieving their goals over long periods, so using the various tools that are available are critical to your success. Our natural tendency is to look at and try new things all the time and have new things that we want to achieve. These new things can be achieved, but they need to go on your overall list of things to do or achieve whilst you stay focused on the goals that you are currently working on. To do this, there are several types of tool that you can use to help you stay focused.

1. **Paper diary/planner systems** were the only tools to use until the late 1980s, when technology started to boom. Planner systems such as Day Timer, Filofax, Franklin Diaries, Debden, Day Runner plus many more enabled you to create your goals and plans of action and then manage your day-to-day activities extremely well. These systems are still available today and are used very successfully by millions of people.

   A lot of people still like using paper-based systems because they like the ability to develop and actually write out their daily To Do List as it helps them to stay on track with getting things done. Writing your goals and activities in a paper system has its positives and negatives – rewriting things all the time can be a tedious process, but on the other hand it can be the most important part of ensuring you achieve your goals.

2. **Electronic diary systems** – with the proliferation of computers, tablet devices and mobile phones, and the ability to synchronise data between them, electronic diaries such as Outlook, iCal, Google Calendar and many other systems enable you to automate the planning process by enabling you to plan your goals and activities and then enter them into the electronic diary.

   The data entered into these diaries can be set up as recurring events, only requiring you to enter them once and have them show up in your daily list automatically when they are due. One of the drawbacks of the automation of this process means you do not have continued focus and can also become slack and relaxed in the day-to-day planning process which is critical to achieving your goals. You need to be aware of this and avoid it.

When using electronic diaries you still need to have the same planning focus that is required when using a paper planning system. A negative of electronic systems is that if there are problems with your computer, you could lose all of your data. Backing up your data is crucial to ensuring that in such an event, you are able to restore back and keep going.

Use of cloud-based systems now make the loss of data far less of an issue and enable you to access the information from a central database from many different devices.

3. **Goal planning and tracking systems** – there is now a multitude of goal planning and tracking systems available, which can be computer-based systems or online systems. Over the years I have tried Goal Pro, Plan Plus Online, Goals on Track, Tiger Goal Setting and Achieve Planner and at present I am trialling Success Wizard, which is proving to be an excellent system. When searching for systems I have seen many more available but I have found that these systems provided most of the services I required.

These goal planning systems enable you to create your goals in various categories and then develop a complete action plan aimed at achieving your goals right down to day-to-day tasks. As with all planning systems, you do need to work the system on a daily basis.

4. **Vision boards** are a great way of keeping your RAS focused on what you want to achieve. A vision board is a collation of pictures, words and sayings that you put together and have located in a place that you can see many times a day. Many successful people will tell you that they always use vision boards as they find it helps them keep on track towards achieving their goals.

5. **Time clock** – when you are working out your daily plan, you create blocks of time for doing things. A time clock enables you to work the time allocated to a task and then move on to the next when it is due. Some may say that that means you don't actually finish a task before you need to move on. The key here is that when you plan your day, you set the time you are allowing for a

particular task based on what you expect to achieve. If you are looking to complete that task fully, then allow the amount of time that is required to complete it. That may be the whole day. If you are working on a project that will take a long to time to complete, you will break it down into smaller tasks and plan to complete those tasks over a period of time. As you plan your day, you will put that task into your day with a specific time plan for working on.

An example of breaking down a project into smaller tasks is writing this book. I have set a project plan and part of the plan is to write for 1½ hours a day starting at 6.00am and finishing at 7.30am. If I have time available later in the day, I can write some more. This plan is based around my current activity schedule and the amount of time that I can productively focus on the task. I can write around 1200 words in this time. I could plan to write for 2, 2½ or 3 hours, but I may not be able to productively focus on the task over the longer time frame. The amount of words I write would be less on a per minute basis as I lose focus. So you need to plan around the time you have available and the amount of time you can productively focus on a task.

6. In today's technological world, there are new **apps and tools** being designed every day to help with all sorts of things in your life. You can research these apps and tools to find which ones suit you the best. But remember, do not continually chop and change. You need to find one that works and stick with it. People who chop and change all the time have a tendency to get nowhere.

There are no doubt many more tools you can use to help you focus on achieving your goals. Take your time and trial several of these products so you can find the ones that suit you. It may be time-consuming to test them but it will be worth it in the long run. I use Outlook as my email, contacts, calendar and task system, so when looking for a goal planning system, I am looking for one that will automatically synchronise the calendar and tasks with Outlook. I also prefer the system to be online so I can access the live database from any device that I am using at the time.

2.6 Celebrate Your Successes

We celebrate birthdays, anniversaries and other specific achievements that happen in our life. We do this to recognise the effort that was put in, to simply say, *"I made it,"* to show our enjoyment of having arrived at that point in time and for many other reasons. So it is important that you recognise your achievements and celebrate them.

At our workshops and coaching groups, I always start the sessions with asking everyone to write down what they have achieved over the past month, quarter, year or even further back. Nearly all attendees attending the workshop or coaching group for the first time struggle to create even a small list of achievements, and yet, when I ask them what are the things they haven't been able to achieve, they can very quickly write a long list of items.

This is because for most people, our brain has a natural tendency to think negatively about things, so we are always focusing on what we haven't done and beating ourselves around the head about it, rather than also thinking about what we have achieved. When the attendees start to focus on what they have actually achieved over the time frame the question relates to, they start to see that there are several items that they have done, and that they have made progress, and generally realise that the issue is that they just have a list of things that haven't been done that is continually growing.

What they also realise is that although there are a lot of things they have achieved, because they do not have a planned structure for what needs to be done to achieve their goals, a lot of the most important tasks have not been done and that is why they are not moving forward at the pace they would like.

So it is important to celebrate your successes, whether big or small; the size of the celebration is relevant to the size of the success. Gaining an important sale could mean you pop a bottle of champagne at dinner, achieving your annual revenue target could mean you take a week's holiday somewhere. What you celebrate and how you celebrate it is up to you; the important things here is when you have a win big or small, celebrate it.

2.7 Where To From Here?

The Time Retriever Time Management Coaching

At The Time Retriever, we have noticed over years of coaching business owners and managers that the biggest issue they have is finding the time to get things done. Although they may have a plan for what they want to do, their days are constantly bombarded with distractions, interruptions, procrastination, etc., resulting in the age-old sayings, *"there's just not enough hours in the day"* and *"I just don't have the time to get things done."*

We believe that when you are able to get control of your time, everything gets done, and your business will grow and you will become very successful.

We offer Time Management Coaching Programs aimed at helping you achieve success. It's not possible to get control of your time by just doing a 1 or 2 day course – you need someone to help you be accountable for making the changes you need to make to your habits and patterns over time.

Our Time Management Coaching Programs are aimed at teaching you what to do and then coaching you over 12 months (or more if necessary), holding you accountable for implementing what you have learned.

Once you start to get control of your time, all of those other important things you need to do, like marketing, sales, recruiting quality people, learning how to lead your team, creating systems and processes aimed at building a business that works without you and investing your profits enabling you to have an enjoyable lifestyle, will all start happening very quickly.

Stop the frustration of not getting things done. Contact us today and let your dreams become your reality.

> **To find out more about The Time Retriever Coaching Program, please contact us on 1300 794 401 or success@timeretrievers.com.au. Visit our website www.timeretrievers.com.au**

APPENDIX

The Time Retriever Templates & Tools

THE TIME RETRIEVER
FINDING YOUR WHY

My Personal Why

My Business Why

Rory Vaden, author of *Take The Stairs* provides these 20 Whats to find Your Why:

1. What amount of money do you want to make?

2. What places would you like to visit in the world?

3. What type of job would you like to do each day?

4. What would your perfect day look like – how would you spend your time, what would you do?

5. What are the characteristics of your perfect spouse?

6. What do you want to look like?

7. What do you want to give back to the world?

8. What do you want to be known for?

9. What are the things you believe in most?

10. What people can help you get to where you want to go?

11. What are the things you would like to have?

12. What are the most exciting things you'd like to try?

13. What events would you like to go to?

14. What type of house do you want to have?

15. What people would you like to meet?

16. What amount of money do you want to have at retirement?

17. What would you do if you knew you couldn't fail?

18. What things would have to happen in order to accomplish that huge dream?

19. What do you want people to think of when they think of you?

20. What people do you want to spend most of your time with?

THE TIME RETRIEVER
VISION STATEMENTS

My Personal Vision

My Business Vision

YOUR 3 KEY GOALS TO SUCCESS
GOAL LIST

PERSONAL GOALS

WHAT	WHEN
3 week holiday Europe	1 year
Weekend on Gold Coast	1 year
Photography course	1 year
Hybrid bike	1 year
Reduce weight to 85kg	1 year
3x5 shed for back yard	2 years
Join football club	1 year
Melbourne cup weekend in Apollo Bay	2 years
5 investment properties	7 years
Family holiday to Disneyland	3 years
Working holiday around Australia	10 years
Tony Robbins 3 day event	2 years

THE TIME RETRIEVER
YOUR 3 KEY GOALS TO SUCCESS
GOAL LIST

BUSINESS GOALS

WHAT	WHEN
$500,000 revenue	
2 new sales reps	
Annual conference	
Replace ute	
Herald Sun Home Show	
HIA Home Show	
Sales training program	
Pat Mesiti Boot Camp	
Paint warehouse	
Develop company operating procedures	
Relocate premises	

YOUR 3 KEY GOALS TO SUCCESS

3 KEY GOALS TO BE ACHIEVED BY   BUSINESS & PERSONAL

1 Achieve $500,000 revenue   30/06/2010

STEPS

• Set budget by month	30/6/2009
• Develop marketing plan	30/6/2009
• Sales training 2 sessions each month – 1st session start by	15/7/2009
• 2 new sales reps 1 in Sept 1 in February	1/9/2009
• Sales leadership competition to start	1/1/2010

2 Develop complete operating procedures for business   30/4/2010

STEPS

• Prepare flow chart for current sales/supply/follow up process	31/7/2009
• Determine what other procedures need to be developed	31/8/2009
• Review current procedure with staff – and start developing new systems	30/9/2009
• Draft of new procedure ready	30/10/2009
• Finalise system documentation/videos	30/11/2009
• Train staff and implement main sales/supply/follow up procedures	30/11/2009
• Develop remaining procedures	30/3/2010
• Finalise train and implement remaining procedures	30/4/2010

3 Relocate to new business premises   31/1/2010

STEPS

• Determine what the criteria for the new premises will be	31/7/2009
• Locate new premises	30/9/2009
• Finalise leasing	30/10/2009
• Plan move	24/12/2009
• Move completed	31/1/2010

THE TIME RETRIEVER

YOUR 3 KEY GOALS TO SUCCESS
GOAL LIST

PERSONAL & BUSINESS GOALS

WHAT   **WHEN**

_____

_____

_____

_____

_____

_____

_____

_____

_____

_____

_____

_____

_____

_____

YOUR 3 KEY GOALS TO SUCCESS

3 KEY GOALS TO BE ACHIEVED BY   BUSINESS & PERSONAL

1

STEPS

_____

_____

_____

_____

2

STEPS

_____

_____

_____

_____

3

STEPS

_____

_____

_____

_____

Sample 12 Month Key Goals

Time Retrievers Pty Ltd
1300 794 401

30th June 2010
$500,000 Revenue
Developed Complete Operating System
Relocated business to new premises
3 week holiday Europe
Achieved 85kgs in weight

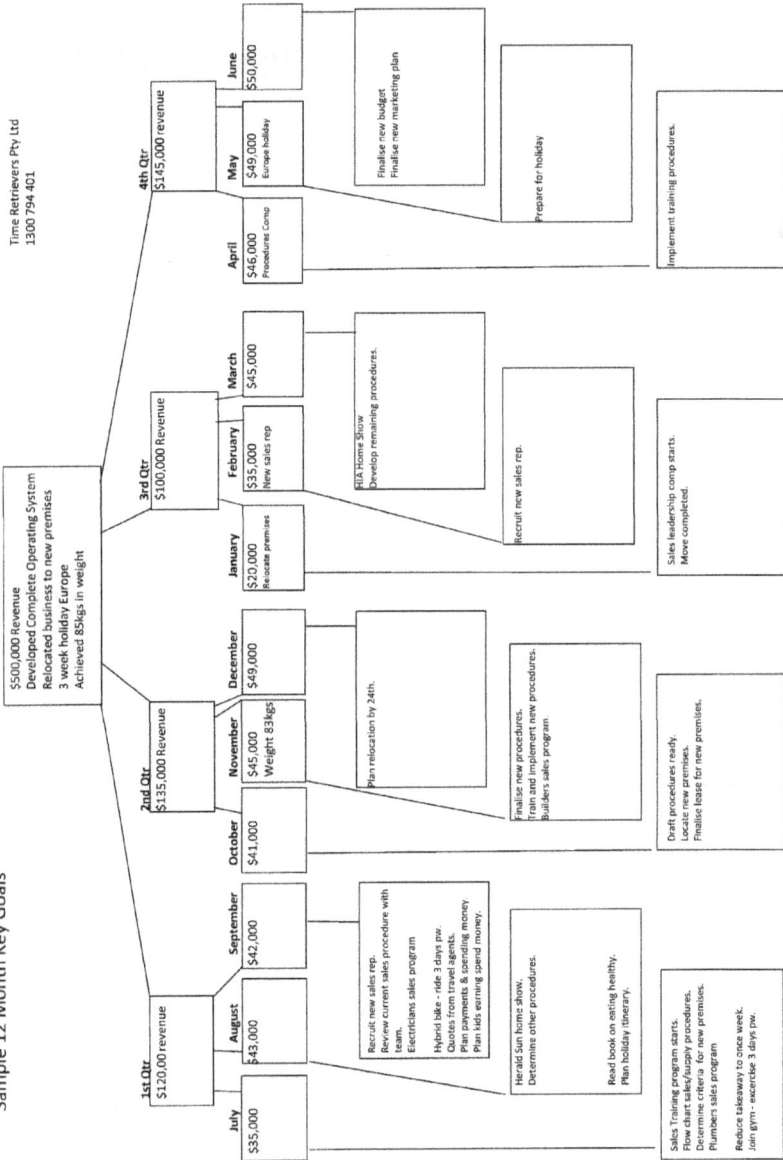

1st Qtr
$120,00 revenue

July	August	September
$35,000	$43,000	$42,000

Recruit new sales rep.
Review current sales procedure with team.
Electricians sales program

Hybrid bike - ride 3 days pw.
Quotes from travel agents.
Plan payments & spending money.
Plan kids earning spend money.

Herald Sun home show.
Determine other procedures.

Read book on eating healthy.
Plan holiday itinerary.

Sales Training program starts.
Flow chart sales/supply procedures.
Determine criteria for new premises.
Plumbers sales program

Reduce takeaway to once week.
Join gym - excercise 3 days pw.

2nd Qtr
$135,000 Revenue

October	November	December
$41,000	$45,000 Weight 83kgs	$49,000

Plan relocation by 24th.

Finalise new procedures.
Train and implement new procedures.
Builder's sales program.

Draft procedures ready.
Locate new premises.
Finalise lease for new premises.

3rd Qtr
$100,000 Revenue

January	February	March
$20,000 Relocate premises	$35,000 New sales rep	$45,000

HIA Home Show
Develop remaining procedures.

Recruit new sales rep.

Sales leadership comp starts.
Move completed.

4th Qtr
$145,000 revenue

April	May	June
$46,000 Procedures Comp	$49,000 Europe holiday	$50,000

Finalise new budget
Finalise new marketing plan

Prepare for holiday

Implement training procedures.

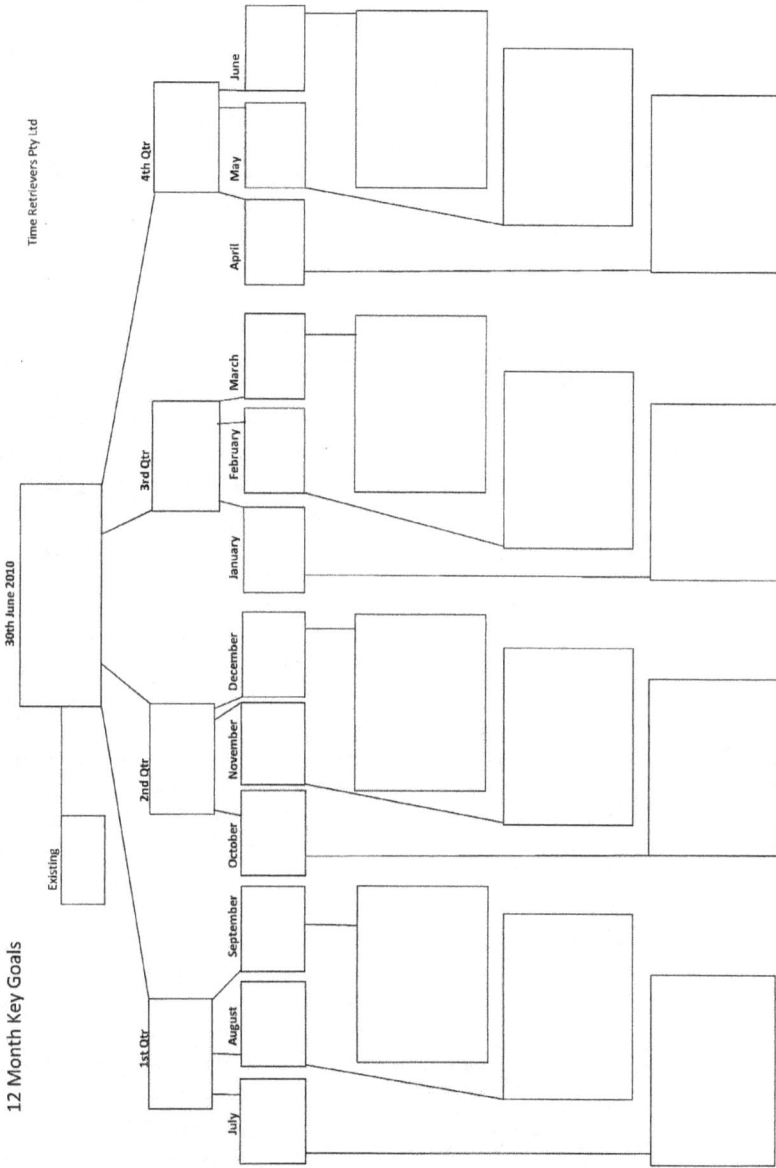

MY BUSINES QUARTERLY PLAN
July - September 2009

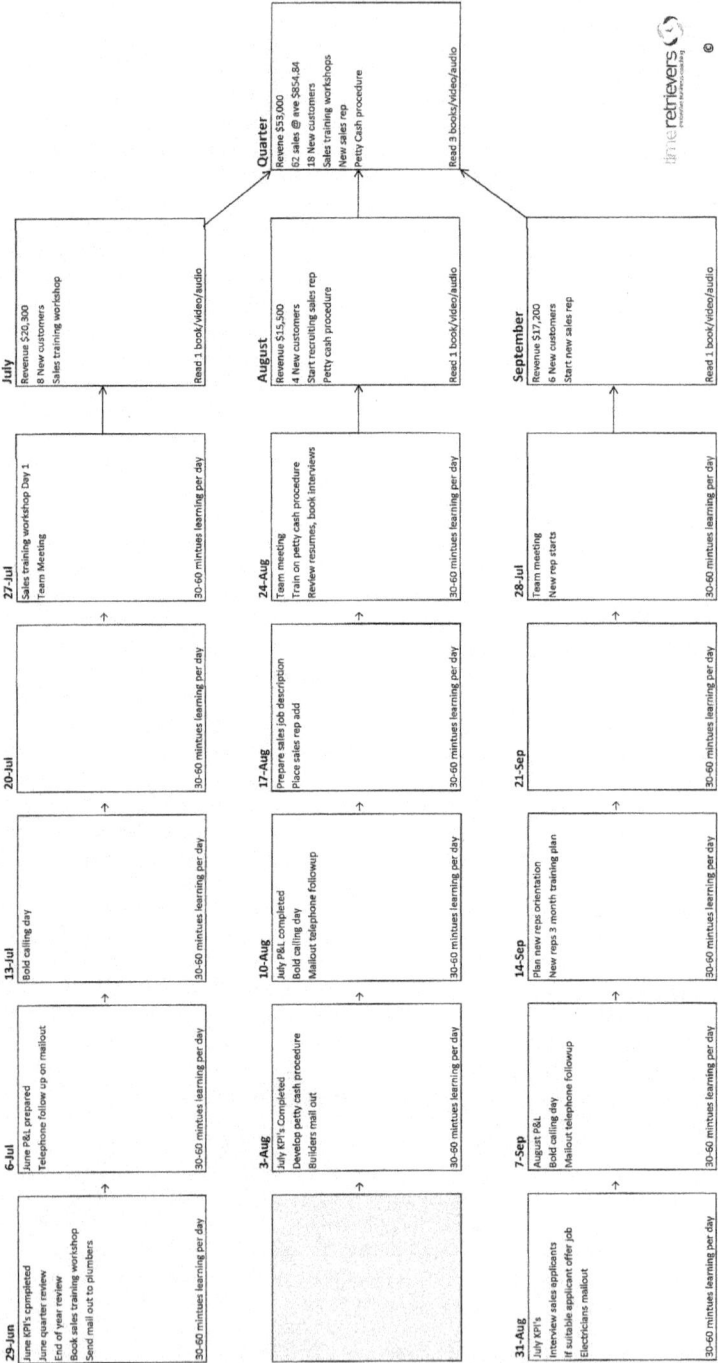

Quarter
Revene $53,000
62 sales @ ave $854,84
18 New customers
Sales training workshops
New sales rep
Petty Cash procedure

Read 3 books/video/audio

July
Revenue $20,300
8 New customers
Sales training workshop

Read 1 book/video/audio

27-Jul
Sales training workshop Day 1
Team Meeting

30-60 mintues learning per day

20-Jul

30-60 mintues learning per day

13-Jul
Bold calling day

30-60 mintues learning per day

6-Jul
June P&L prepared
Telephone follow up on mailout

30-60 mintues learning per day

29-Jun
June KPI's completed
June quarter review
End of year review
Book sales training workshop
Send mail out to plumbers

30-60 mintues learning per day

August
Revenue $15,500
4 New customers
Start recruiting sales rep
Petty cash procedure

Read 1 book/video/audio

24-Aug
Team meeting
Train on petty cash procedure
Review resumes, book interviews

30-60 mintues learning per day

17-Aug
Prepare sales job description
Place sales rep add

30-60 mintues learning per day

10-Aug
July KPI's completed
Bold calling day
Mailout telephone followup

30-60 mintues learning per day

3-Aug
July KPI's Completed
Develop petty cash procedure
Builders mail out

30-60 mintues learning per day

September
Revenue $17,200
6 New customers
Start new sales rep

Read 1 book/video/audio

28-Jul
Team meeting
New rep starts

30-60 mintues learning per day

21-Sep

30-60 mintues learning per day

14-Sep
Plan new reps orientation
New reps 3 month training plan

30-60 mintues learning per day

7-Sep
August P&L
Bold calling day
Mailout telephone followup

30-60 mintues learning per day

31-Aug
July KPI's
Interview sales applicants
If suitable applicant offer job
Electricians mailout

30-60 mintues learning per day

Key Focus Points -   4.1 New sales per week

1.2 New customers per week

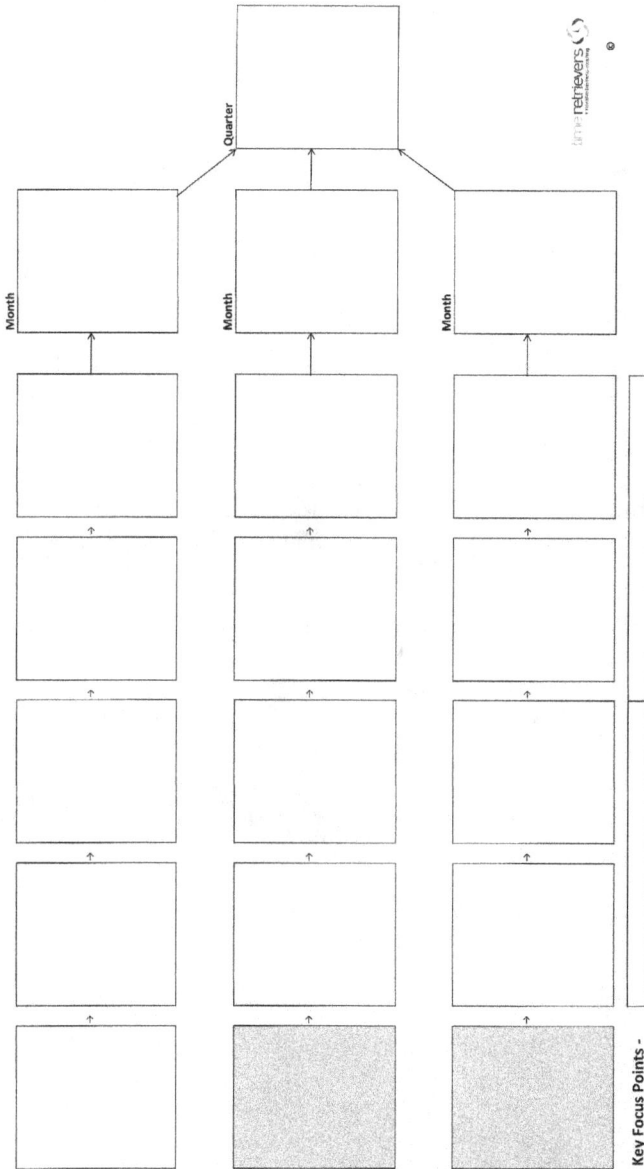

MY BUSINESS QUARTERLY PLAN
Jan - Mar 2011

Quarter

Month

Month

Month

Key Focus Points -

Default Diary

Company Name

Time	Sunday	Monday	Tuesday	Wednesday	Thursday	Friday	Saturday
7:00 AM to 7:30 AM							
7:30 AM to 8:00 AM							
8:00 AM to 8:15 AM							
8:15 AM to 8:30 AM							
8:30 AM to 8:45 AM		Appointments	Phone Calls	Proposal development	Appointments	Phone Calls	
8:45 AM to 9:00 AM		Appointments	Phone Calls	Proposal development	Appointments	Phone Calls	
9:00 AM to 9:15 AM		Appointments	Phone Calls	Proposal development	Appointments	Phone Calls	
9:15 AM to 9:30 AM		Appointments	Phone Calls	Proposal development	Appointments	Phone Calls	
9:30 AM to 9:45 AM		Appointments	Phone Calls	Appointments	Appointments	Phone Calls	
9:45 AM to 10:00 AM		Phone Calls		Appointments	Appointments	Phone Calls	
10:00 AM to 10:15 AM		Phone Calls		Appointments	Appointments	Phone Calls	
10:15 AM to 10:30 AM		Phone Calls		Appointments	Appointments	Phone Calls	
10:30 AM to 10:45 AM		Phone Calls		Appointments	Proposal development		
10:45 AM to 11:00 AM					Proposal development		
11:00 AM to 11:15 AM					Proposal development		
11:15 AM to 11:30 AM					Proposal development		
11:30 AM to 11:45 AM			Appointments		Proposal development	Cold Calling	
11:45 AM to 12:00 PM			Appointments		Proposal development	Cold Calling	
12:00 PM to 1:00 PM			Appointments			Cold Calling	
1:00 PM to 1:15 PM		Cold Calling	Appointments			Cold Calling	
1:15 PM to 1:30 PM		Cold Calling	Appointments			Cold Calling	
1:30 PM to 1:45 PM		Cold Calling	Appointments			Cold Calling	
1:45 PM to 2:00 PM		Cold Calling	Appointments	Proposal development			
2:00 PM to 2:15 PM		Cold Calling	Appointments	Proposal development			
2:15 PM to 2:30 PM		Cold Calling	Appointments	Proposal development			
2:30 PM to 2:45 PM			Appointments	Proposal development			
2:45 PM to 3:00 PM			Appointments	Proposal development	Phone Calls	Invoicing	
3:00 PM to 3:15 PM			Invoicing	Proposal development	Phone Calls	Follow up	
3:15 PM to 3:30 PM			Follow up	Proposal development	Phone Calls	Office follow up	
3:30 PM to 3:45 PM			Office follow up	Proposal development	Phone Calls		
3:45 PM to 4:00 PM				Proposal development	Phone Calls		
4:00 PM to 4:15 PM						Plan Next Week	Exercise
4:15 PM to 4:30 PM						Plan Next Week	
4:30 PM to 4:45 PM						Plan Next Week	
4:45 PM to 5:00 PM						Plan Next Week	
EVENING ACTIVITIES		Plan tomorrow / Personal Development / Exercise	Plan tomorrow / Personal Development	Plan tomorrow / Personal Development / Exercise	Plan tomorrow / Personal Development	Plan tomorrow / Personal Development / Exercise	

Default Diary

time retrievers
innovative business coaching

TO DO LIST

Priority	Activity	Due Date	How Long to Do?	Who Will Do It?	Done

THE TIME RETRIEVER
DAILY PLANNING CHECKLIST

> **"Never start your day until it is finished"**
> *Jim Rohn*

The cornerstone of success is clearly understanding what you need to do on a daily basis, and ensuring that you complete the things that you have determined are important to your success. Once you have set your goals and created your action plan, it is now time to work with your plan on a weekly and daily basis.

Have you ever woken up multiple times during the early hours of the morning with your mind going flat out thinking about the things that you need to do? And when you finally got out of bed, you were still tired and when you go to write down all of the things that kept waking you up, you can't remember what they were? This is because your brain is in alarm mode and is actively trying to keep everything in place for you for tomorrow, preventing you from having a good night's sleep.

To counteract this, your daily planning should be done the night before. You select a time late in the day when you sit down and prepare your plan for tomorrow. Once it is completed and when you go to bed, your brain will have the security of knowing that you won't forget anything and your subconscious mind now takes over and works on how you will complete your planned activities. This is in a totally different area of the brain, and it does not disturb your night's sleep.

Remember, there is no such thing as "time management." Time is simply taken up with a series of activities one after another. Everything you do is an activity. The only way to manage and make the best use of your time is to manage the activities, ensuring that your most important activities actually get done. So, what is a daily plan? In a daily plan, you determine what activities you need to carry out the next day and then list them in priority of importance, with the most important activities being your A1, A2, A3, etc. activities. Some activities (appointments, etc.) may have specific times allocated to them.

Another important part of creating success in your life is forming good habits. When you talk with people that have had great success in their lives, they will always talk about the things that they habitually do, things like exercise every day, make a specific number of phone calls every day, plan every day. To create the success you are looking for, you will need to create specific habits in your day. This is not always easy: a study carried out by NASA in the 1950s-60s revealed that it takes 21 to 30 days of consistently doing the same thing to create a new habit. If you miss just one day, it starts back at day one again. You will need to have the faith and determination to make this succeed.

The following Time Retriever Daily Planning Checklist provides you with a template for planning your day. Its purpose is to help you create the habit of planning each day and also provides you with a methodology for planning each day. Use it for at least 30 consecutive days to help you establish your new planning habit.

The Time Retriever Daily Planning Checklist is a part of the Time Retriever Time Management and Business Coaching Program. These programs are delivered through our planning workshops and various business coaching packages.

This checklist is created in three sections; the first section is the list of items/information required for the planning process, the second section is the planning process at the end of the day, and the third section is the morning review of your plan prior to taking action.

SECTION ONE

Items/information required to plan your day

To create a daily plan you need to have all of the information at hand. This information will come from:

1. Your diary – whether you use a paper or electronic diary, it will have your current day's plan, showing what has been completed and what is still outstanding. It will also contain your notes from the day that may need further action.

2. Your current day's To Do List if this is separate from your diary. Again it will show what has been completed and what is still outstanding.

3. Rolling To Do List – a rolling To Do List is your list of things that you need to action, from which you will select items for the next day's plan.

4. Your noting system – people keep notes from their day in various methods: notepads, Evernote, notes in Outlook, etc. Your notes from today are required to see if there are any actions that need to be taken from the day's events.

5. Goals System – you need to have your goals available for you to review, so it is always a good practice to have your whole goals planning system with you when you review your day.

6. Email – you will need to have access to your emails to review any action that needs to be taken from them.

7. Vision Board system – have your vision board available for your review to help you keep focused on what you want to achieve. This can be an electronic or printed version. It may also be a part of your goals planning system.

8. Check family events – prior to planning tomorrow, it is wise to check with family members so you are aware of what events they have tomorrow that may involve you.

9. Production schedule – if you are in a production environment, you may need you production schedule for tomorrow to ensure you cover all aspects of your business.

You may have other items specific to you that need to be added to this list.

SECTION TWO

The Night Before

Planning your day should only take 10 to 15 minutes. You could have a set time frame to do your planning: 5.00pm, or the last activity you do before finishing your work day, or it may be later in the evening.

1. Using your diary, notes and To Do List, review the events of today; reflect back on what happened and what you achieved. Most people never think about what they have achieved – they are too busy beating themselves around the head about what they didn't get done. Give yourself a congratulatory pat on the back for what you did actually achieve.

2. Review what is already in your diary for tomorrow. You may have appointments already planned; there may even be events you are attending. Confirm they are still on.

3. The next step is to create a list of activities that need to be completed tomorrow. Remember, the amount of activities you will be able to carry out will be dependent on what you already have in your diary and the amount of time it takes to complete each activity. It makes no sense to plan activities that cannot realistically be completed in the day.

a. Review the items from today's To Do List – do the items that were not completed need to be added to tomorrow or another day? Add the items that need to be completed tomorrow to the list and move the other items that are not completed to your rolling To Do List. (If you use an electronic diary, you can move them to the day you intend to do them on. There may also be items already listed for tomorrow.)

b. Check your Weekly Plan – are there activities that are scheduled for this week that need to be completed tomorrow? If yes, add them to the list.

c. Check your rolling To Do List to see if there are items on the list that need to be completed tomorrow. Add them to the list.

d. Check your notes from today's activities – are there any actions that need to be carried out tomorrow as a result of these activities? Add them to the list. If there are actions that need to be carried out at a later date, move them to your rolling To Do List or enter them into your electronic To Do List for that day. (Time Tip – always number the notes you make 1, 2, 3, 4, etc. When you plan an action for them in your To Do List, you then title your activity with the date and note number to refer back to, i.e. you might have a note from the 28th December No 2 that says, "contact Matthew &

Jane to arrange meeting on the 7ᵗʰ January." When you create your To Do List activity, it will look like this – Arrange meeting (28/12 No 2) – this now refers you back to note No 2 in your notes from the 28ᵗʰ December.)

e. **Check with your family members** about events that you may be involved in tomorrow.

4. **Now you have your list of activities** prepared for tomorrow, you will need to prioritise them in order from the most important to the least important. The easiest way to do this is using the A, B, C method:

a. An "A" activity has a high priority and must be done – it is really important to you or the business. These are items that are a key part of implementing your action plan.

b. A "B" activity is an activity that needs to be done, but is not as important as the "A" activities.

c. A "C" activity is something that would be nice to do, but if it does not get done, does not create a problem.

Once you have categorised them into A's, B's & C's, look at your As and number them in order of importance A1, A2, A3, etc. Sometimes it is hard to decide the level of importance between each activity. You can ask yourself, "*which one will help me achieve my most important goal?*" and give it the highest priority. Or simply make a decision and work with it. You're a's should be completed first. Once you have completed the As you then do the same with the B's and C's.

5. **Now look at your diary and create blocks of time** in your day when the activities will be carried out. The A's should always be in the first blocks. You will need to understand your own attention span and create blocks of activities to match. I

know that I can stay focused for around 1½ hours and then need a break. So I will plan my day with a 1½ hour time block for doing my As. I plan an easy and enjoyable task for around 10 to 15 minutes in between (coffee, make phone calls, etc.).

At times you're a's may be time-related, i.e. you may need to complete a report that is urgent, but won't have the information available until after 1.00pm. You would plan a block of time starting at 1.30pm and set your alarm for this time. Irrespective of what you are doing, you will start working on the A item until it is finished.

Multitasking is a load of rubbish; the way to create success is to prioritise your time and focus on completing the one task you have at hand. In one of our coaching sessions, a client who had been trying to merge and clean out his database over a period of 18 months stated how he allocated the time to carry out this task and whilst doing it found it was taking considerably longer than he had planned. He decided to stay with the task until it was completed, even though in the back of his mind he was thinking of other items he really needed to do. As he said, it felt so good to finally have the job completed and off his list. When he went to the next task, he no longer had a part of his mind thinking about completing it. He also had the bonus of now having his database completely ready for marketing.

One task completed is far better than multiple tasks half completed.

Your day is now planned and ready to go.

6. **Now go to your goals system and review your goals** – use your vision board to go through each one, read it out aloud, look at your picture of the goal, and visualise yourself having achieved it. Doing this on a daily basis establishes it firmly into your subconscious mind, enabling it to focus on helping you achieve those goals.

SECTION THREE

First Thing Each Day

First thing next morning you need to review your plan. If you have an exercise routine planned for the start of each day, you will review your plan after you have completed your exercise.

1. **Review your plan for the day** and adjust where necessary. You may have received information overnight that requires you to make changes to your plan.

2. **Now go to your goals system and review your goals** – use your vision board to go through each one, read it out aloud, look at your picture of the goal, and visualise yourself having achieved it. Doing this on a daily basis establishes it firmly into your subconscious mind, enabling it to focus on helping you achieve those goals.

3. **It is now time to get into Action** – start working on your highest priority item on your to do list.

DISTRACTIONS

We are now at the point where most people strike problems with carrying out their plan. The day is planned with all good intentions, but when you try to start working on your tasks, everything starts to get in the way, and at the end of the day, you might have a To Do List with only a few items done (generally not the number one item) or nothing done at all. So what do you do? I have seen plenty of people that have said, "*I tried that and it doesn't work.*" What a load of rubbish – they mostly tried it once and on that day it didn't work.

It is very rare that you will make this work on the first, second or even third day. You can be very experienced at this process and there will still be days when things just go wrong. That's life. You need to keep working with it until you master it. To learn how to deal with distractions, contact us at Time Retrievers and find out about our Distraction Buster process.

DAILY PLANNING CHECKLIST

Creating the habit of preparing your daily plan is critical to creating your success. At the end of each day you prepare your plan for tomorrow.

Check off that you have at hand the following items required to prepare your plan:

☐	Diary (paper/electronic)	☐	Your noting system (Evernote, notepad, diary, etc.)
☐	Email		
☐	Today's To Do List	☐	Production Schedule (if required)
☐	Vision Board (paper/electronic)		
☐	Rolling To Do List	☐	Goals System (Weekly Plan, Quarterly Action Plan, Goals List, etc.)
☐	Check family events		

The Night Before

Check off the following steps required to plan your day:

1. Review today's achievements
2. Review tomorrow's diary
3. Create a list of activities that need to be completed tomorrow: To Do List (these activities will come from)
   a. Items not completed today
   b. Actions from your Weekly Plan
   c. Items from your Rolling To Do List
   d. Items from yesterday's notes
   e. family events/activities
4. Prioritise the Actions on your To Do list (use the A,B,C or 1,2,3 methods)
5. Block out time segments in your diary when these activities will be completed
6. Review each of your goals using your vision board system

First Thing Each Day

1. Review your plan for today and adjust where necessary
2. Review your goals using your vision board system
3. Action the No 1 item on your To Do List

THE TIME RETRIEVER

DISTRACTION BUSTER GUIDE

If you have planned your day, there is nothing more frustrating than having your plan totally destroyed due to constant distractions and interruptions.

As a business owner or manager, the daily planning process needs to include the question, *"what are the things that will interrupt my ability to focus on completing my highest priority activities?"* When these items are determined, you can add the elimination of them to your goals and then create a plan of action aimed at eliminating them.

Simply blocking out the distractions and interruptions is also not as easy as it may seem. The whole environment that you have created around you over time has led to these distractions and interruptions having a constant effect on your time.

To identify these distractions, you will need to keep track of what they are. The Time Retriever Distraction Buster Tracking Form is designed to enable you to determine what your distractions are, the frequency of their occurrence and which ones you will need to plan to eliminate first.

I developed this method may years ago when I first started my management career, and utilise it every time I notice that distractions are creeping back into my day. The Distraction Buster is a part of the Time Retrievers Time Management and Business Coaching programs. It is designed to help you eliminate distractions and interruptions in your day-to-day life.

THE DISTRACTION BUSTER FORMULA

STEP 1.

When you start your day, print out a copy of the Time Retriever Distraction Buster Tracking Form, and ensure you put the day and date on the top of the form.

To enable you to record the distraction details, the Time Retriever Distraction Buster Tracking Form has 4 columns, entitled:

1. **Time**	the time you are distracted
2. **Who distracted you**	the person or thing that distracted you
3. **Business Area**	what part of the business they work in, sales, admin etc
4. **Describe the distraction**	write down a description of what the distraction was

As you start working on your planned activities and get disrupted, note down on the tracker:

1. The time you were distracted
2. Who distracted you
3. What area of the business they are in
4. Why they distracted you

If you were not even able to start working on items in your plan, note down on the tracker why you were unable to start.

On the bottom of the form are codes relating to the business areas that can be used in the tracker. You may like to add more codes to suit you.

STEP 2.

After 2 weeks, collect each of the daily tracker forms, analyse the data and create a list of the key reasons you were distracted during each day.

STEP 3.

Prioritise the list with the item that distracted you the most at the top of the list through to the item that distracted you the least at the bottom of the list.

STEP 4.

Select the No 1 distraction from your list and determine why it is constantly distracting you. Then create a plan of action to eliminate it. Work through the list one at a time eliminating as many of the distractions as you can.

Some of these distractions may take some time to eliminate and you will need to add the elimination of them to your quarterly plans.

Some sample distractions and elimination plans are:

1. A sales representative may be constantly coming to you to ask questions about a product or asking for permission to discount pricing, etc. Once you have identified this, your action plan may be:

   a. Arrange for them to be fully trained on the product that they sell. This training may be carried out by you, by another staff member or the product supplier.

   b. Meet with the sales rep and let them know that it is their responsibility to ensure that they know the product fully and not have to ask questions all the time.

   c. You may have to decide that you need to let go of some of the sales process and give the sales rep more authority to make decisions about selling the product.

2. The tracker may show that you micromanage the business and that no one is allowed to do anything without talking to you. If you are a micromanager of your business, and cannot let go, your business will not grow to its potential. You will eventually burn out and your business will have a lower sale value should you decide to sell it. When you identify this, your plan may be:

   a. Decide to learn how to delegate more tasks and provide more authority to your team.

   b. Source a leadership training course for yourself to learn more about managing your team effectively.

   c. Attend the course and implement your new knowledge and skills.

3. The tracker may show that the employees you have recruited are not at the standard required to carry out their roles. This would suggest your recruitment skills need to be further enhanced. Your action plan would be:

   a. Source a recruitment training workshop.

   b. Implement the new recruitment knowledge and skills into your business.

4. The tracker may show that you are constantly interrupted by customers. Your action plan may be:

   a. If you have a sales or customer service team, advise them that all new customers must be handled by them.

   b. All existing customers that want to deal directly with you are gradually weaned off onto your team members.

As you work with this tracker, you will start to see that more than 60% of the interruptions are created because, although you may be a business owner or manager, there has been very little development of your business management skills. It will show you what skills you will need to develop further, and if you work on developing these skills, you will see the amount of distractions reduced considerably and your business grow and become more successful with less day-to-day interaction by you.

It will also show you that your own mindset can be the biggest distraction in your day. Thoughts such as:

a. "I feel tired so I'll do it after a rest"

b. "I have got some time, I will do it this afternoon"

c. "I really don't feel like doing it right now"

d. "This will take too long, I will do these other things first"

e. The subconscious thoughts of, "firing them is hard, I will do it on Friday afternoon."

All of these thoughts need to be entered into the Distraction Tracker to enable you to truly identify the real distractions in your day.

This process is purely about identifying and creating a plan to eliminate distractions in your day. In the Time Retriever Time Management Formula, there are other strategies that you can utilise to ensure you get control of your day and do the important things in your business. Visit our website or contact us to find out how the Time Retriever Formula can help you become an even more successful person.

THE TIME RETRIEVER DISTRACTION BUSTER TOOL

List all items that distract you whilst you are endeavouring to complete an important task from your To Do List. If you had a set time to start, and did not get started, write down what stopped you from working on the important task. Also include items such as getting coffee, going to the toilet and where your own discipline failed you.

Day: **Date:**   **Time Started:**   **Time Finished:**

Time	Who Distracted You	Business Area	Describe the Distraction

Codes for Business Area: C – Customer • S – Sales skills • P – Product knowledge • F – Finances • Pe – Personal • A – Administration • Sy – System issues • W – Warehousing • L – Lack of concentration • X – My Headspace/Motivation

Over time, you will be able to determine exactly what distracts you and take action to eliminate these distractions, resulting in you being able to complete your most important tasks.

IT DOESN'T END HERE

The more we work with our clients, the more we learn and see more ways and methods of achieving success through having control of of our day.

As we develop these new methods and ways of getting control of our day, Peter Johnson – The Time Retriever will be constantly documenting them a making them available as downloads on our websites.

To keep yourself up to date with these new methods, we encourage you to make sure you regularly visit our websites

www.timeretrievers.com.au or

www.peterjohnsonauthorspeaker.com

to read our blogs and download the new methods, templates and tools.

All templates mentioned in this book are also available in digital format from

www.timeretrievers.com.au and

www.peterjohnsonauthorspeaker.com.

ABOUT PETER JOHNSON

Principal at **The Time Retriever** coaching and training enterprise, Peter is a testament to a well managed life. For nearly 30 years, in senior management roles and running several businesses, Peter was seen by his staff and colleagues as someone who has 'mastered time'. Shortage of time is the battle cry for many, whether in their business or personal lives. "There are only 24 hours in a day. I just can't get it all done," appeared to be the number one complaint everywhere he worked. Because he was better than most, his staff and colleagues would ask for his advice in how they could better manage theirs. After years of coaching dozens of people, he turned his experience, expertise and passion into a viable business. Peter is now a much sought after coach, trainer and speaker. There are no secrets to successful time management. You can't add hours to the day, but you can learn to prioritize, develop effective ways to say no to distractions and interruptions, take charge of your life and accomplish the things that really matter. Peter enjoys helping others get out of poor time habits and bring huge improvements to their work and their lives. His engaging presentations espouse the principles that make him an effective coach and trainer. His relaxed and interactive style makes him an commanding and influential speaker.

Qualifications and accomplishments

- **Diploma of Management**
- **Certified in supervision, small business management and training and assessment**
- **Certified in Assessment of Informal Learning**
- **Telstra Business of the Year nominee**

As a business coach

In both one on one and group sessions, our coaching is designed to improve business structures and strategies, so you can focus on being the business, not running the business. Based on proven productivity indicators, we help you develop the action plans to manage both the daily and long-term objectives of your business and personal life.

As a trainer/facilitator

The training is driven by the knowledge gained from years of listening to clients and staff and hearing the same complaints about 'not getting it done'. Running a business requires skills that are different from managing people. Learning the difference and maintaining a balance is what gives you 'time' to do both well. That's what our programs are about. And we take the time to do it well.

TRAINING PROGRAMS

Coaching

A coaching strategy built on a foundation of 'the 4 inescapable components of controlling your day' – planning, time management, self discipline, and people management skills that will help you stop procrastinating, use resources effectively and delegate in order to become an effective leader.

Time Management

The Time Retriever Time Management intensive workshop is designed to help you appreciate the importance of time management. This 1 day intensive workshop will:

- **Develop proven time management techniques and strategies**
- **Provide the templates and process for a quarterly action plan**
- **Improve effective self and people management skills to help take control of your day**
- **Start the process for a longer term accountability coaching sessions**

Step 2: The Time Retriever 12 Month Time Management Group Coaching Program is designed to implement the skills learned in the Time Management Intensive. Using the good habits and practicing the skills will bring extraordinary results. Coaching keeps you focused and accountable for the targets you set for yourself.

Sales

Sales training is not just about how to get the sale and close the sale. It's about how to do it efficiently and effectively. Patience and timing are the most critical ingredients in closing sales. Ensuring that your time is spent well is your responsibility. We show you how. You will:

- **Learn to break down your sales targets into easily achievable goals**
- **Identify the activities essential for better results**
- **Identify priorities for maximum results.**

Management Training

Managing people and managing projects are about managing time. We show you how you can do both well by managing your time...not others. You will:

- **Build communication skills for clarity and influence**
- **Create daily plans through focused prioritization**
- **Learn self-discipline skills to reduce constant interruptions and distractions.**

As a speaker

Peter's focus is on the success factors needed to effectively manage your time and your life. Time management is the catch all for the need for control. But without the foundational skills of self management and using available resources, both people and tools, just ticking off a 'to do list' becomes a waste of time. In talks and workshops, participants develop the skills to change habits and patterns.

SPEAKING TOPICS

- **Manage what's important to you**
- **Time management success skills**
- **Learning to say 'No'**
- **The Power of Setting Realistic Goals**
- **A To Do List Is A Waste of Time**
- **Turn Time Into Sales**
- **Business Mum's and The Time Trap**
- **The Admin Time Machine**
- **Control My Day, Managing Childcare? You've Got To Be Kidding Me!**
- **Time and Action As A Network Marketer**

"Peter Johnson of The Time Retriever presented at our 2014 and 2015 conferences on the subjects of both time management and marketing. He is a warm and engaging presenter with a very strong knowledge base and a wealth of experience to provide real life examples to his audience. Delegates who have attended Peter's sessions have overwhelmingly given positive feedback and have gone on to engage Peter in a private capacity. I have found Peter a delight to work with and a valuable addition to our conference programs. I have no hesitation in recommending Peter."

Philippa Valder, Australian Childcare Alliance Victoria